We love God because He  devotion to Him will alway uinely behold His heart for us. In this wonderfully inspiring new book, Daniel invites us to refresh our view of God, and in particular, our perception of how He sees us. Whether a long-time believer or brand new to the Christian faith, these life-giving pages invite us into a deeper encounter with the God who truly delights in His children.

— Matt Redman
Worship leader/songwriter

I have known Daniel since he was a teenager. In all the intervening years the pursuit of intimacy with God has been his magnificent obsession. This wonderful book is the fruit of that pursuit. It is full of revelation and insight into the amazing love of God. Reading this will inspire, challenge, comfort, and heal you.

— Mike Pilavachi
Founder and director, Soul Survivor

Daniel's life has continually modeled a courage and obedience that is a modern picture of the biblical gospel! Sacrifice and joy flowing from a deep intimacy with Jesus. Passion fueled by deep love from and towards Jesus!

— Andy Byrd
Co-founder, Fire and Fragrance Ministries, YWAM Kona

We have a great God and a great gospel. So much of the time we hide in the shadows of shame and distance. What my friend Daniel has written in this book will shatter that shame by inviting you into the exhilarating nearness of the Father who loves you in spite of your failures, just because you're His own.

— Lou Engle
Founder, TheCall

Staying connected to the love of our Father in heaven is a lifeline and anchor that determines the direction of our life decisions. Daniel's book, *Loved*, is a must-read for anyone who needs to ask the question, "Does God really love me?" and get truly connected to the Father. Using his own journey, Daniel helps to uncover the questions we all have that can hinder our connection, and he simply but powerfully declares the truth that can restore us! I highly recommend this book!

— Laura Hackett Park
Worship leader and songwriter, IHOPKC

Nothing is more foundational to our lives than the revelation of God as Father and His amazing love for us. Sadly, though we hear lots of people preach on this message and write on this message, very few actually live in this message. Daniel Hoogteijling is one of these few. I love Daniel because he manifests the nature of the Father and His love like few people I know. He doesn't just write and speak on this subject, but lives it. I've seen it in his life, his family, his relationships and have felt the power of revelation come out of him when he speaks on it. The revelation in the book you are about to read is going to blow your mind. After this book, you will see God in a way you have never seen Him before. You will see yourself in a way you've never seen yourself. You will redefine success in your life as being loved by God and loving Him, and you will see holiness go from a cuss word into an expression of love. Take your time with this book, and let its truth transform you.

— Corey Russell
Speaker and author of *Prayer*, *The Glory Within*, and *Inheritance*

Daniel Hoogteijling is a gifted minister who lives out the gospel the way they did in Acts. *Loved* is an inspiration and challenge to live outside yourself and, as Paul said, be compelled by love. I highly recommend this book.

— Robby Dawkins
International evangelist, author, and speaker

In *Loved*, Daniel has given us an eye-opening glimpse into the fascinating, out-of-this-world love that God has for each of us. I was deeply moved by his transparency about his own struggles to know and experience God as his Father. Daniel's journey into God's heart is truly an invitation for all of us to allow Father to embrace us even in our struggles and weakness so we can know the joy and freedom of being His sons and daughters. I highly recommend this book!

— S. J. Hill
Author of *Enjoying God, A Love for the Ages,* and *What's God Really Like?*

I have watched Daniel's leadership at IHOPKC for the last 7 years. He has been one of our most exceptional leaders. Year after year, his team has displayed the highest character, the deepest humility with glad hearts to serve, and a joyous and contagious love for the gospel. This book reveals the secret behind his leadership. He has given himself to understanding the core of God's wonderful heart. God is love! I am so thankful that Daniel has given himself to understanding God's love and displaying it for all to know. I love this book! It should become a classic read for every believer and every church discipleship program.

— Allen Hood
Associate Director, International House of Prayer, Kansas City

Daniel Hoogteijling carries revelation of the Father's heart as deeply as anyone I know. His commitment to prayer and intimacy with God over many years has forged in him a rich reservoir of understanding of God's love. I'm grateful that he has taken from that reservoir and offered us fresh insights into God's heart. I encourage you to read this book with an open heart and a prayerful mind. I know your heart will be greatly enlarged through the revelation he shares.

— Billy Humphrey
Founder, International House of Prayer Atlanta
Author of *Unceasing* and *The Culture of the Kingdom*

Daniel Hoogteijling has an amazing ability to share the truths of the gospel in a way that melts the heart. Prepare to receive the love of God in a way that makes His affections accessible, meaningful, and life changing. You're about to see your heavenly Father in a marvelously new way.

— Bob Sorge
Author, *Secrets of the Secret Place*

We are fans of Daniel Hoogteijling. As a missionary, Daniel has been fearless to bring God's love to some of the most dangerous places on earth. He is one of the truest people we know. He has great authority to write about the love of God because he lives what he writes. There is safety in being rooted and grounded in the love of God (Eph. 3:17). We are more courageous when we know that nothing, not even our deepest failures, can separate us from God's love. This is one of the most important books you will ever read on your way to having satisfaction and success in your walk with God.

— Wesley and Stacey Campbell
Authors of *Praying the Bible*

Daniel has been a friend of mine for over a decade now. He has consistently provoked me by his passion for God and the deep revelation he carries of the love of the Father. This revelation has sustained him through many trials, and I have seen him persevere in faith over and over again. When we first launched our missions training program, Daniel was on our team and was adamant that the primary revelation necessary for the sustainability of long-term ministry work is a heart that has encountered the love of God. He has not wavered from this truth, and his character, passion, intercession, ministry impact, and deep authentic love for people is the tangible fruit of the love of God at work in his life. The message of this book is powerful and necessary. Let it strike your heart.

— Brian Kim
Founder, Antioch Center for Training and Sending (ACTS)

Living in the Middle East as missionaries to the Muslim world, we are eternally grateful for our beloved friend, Daniel's, message on the love of God. It is one thing to theologically understand that God loves us. However, having confidence in God's unwavering love for us, even in our weakest moments, has been life changing. The truths laid before you in this book are for people in all stages in their walk with Christ. We have made them our bedrock, and they have given us boldness in our assignment among the unreached. One of the many things we love about Daniel is that he truly embodies this message, and thus God has anointed him to share it. As you read this book, we believe you will encounter the love of God in a new way and be delivered from shame which hinders your walk with Him; and in return, you will be equipped to wholeheartedly love God and others in a new way.

— Missionaries among the unreached

LOVED

When the One Who Knows You the Best LOVES YOU THE MOST

DANIEL HOOGTEIJLING

FORERUNNER PUBLISHING

KANSAS CITY, MISSOURI

Loved—When the One Who Knows You the Best Loves You the Most
by Daniel Hoogteijling

Published by Forerunner Publishing
International House of Prayer
3535 E. Red Bridge Road
Kansas City, Missouri 64137
ihopkc.org/books

© Copyright 2019 by Daniel Hoogteijling
All rights reserved. Published 2019

This book or any parts of this book may not be reproduced in any form, stored in a retrieval system, or transmitted in any form by any means—electronic, mechanical, photocopy, recording, or otherwise—without prior written permission of the publisher, except as provided by United States of America copyright law.

Forerunner Publishing is the book-publishing division of the International House of Prayer of Kansas City, an evangelical missions organization that exists to partner in the Great Commission by advancing 24/7 prayer and proclaiming the beauty of Jesus and His glorious return.

ISBN: 978-1-938060-49-6
eBook ISBN: 978-1-938060-50-2

Unless otherwise noted, all Scripture quotations are taken from the New King James Version®. Copyright © 1982 by Thomas Nelson. Used by permission. All rights reserved. Scripture quotations marked (NIV) are taken from the Holy Bible, New International Version®, NIV®. Copyright © 1973, 1978, 1984, 2011 by Biblica, Inc.™ Used by permission of Zondervan. All rights reserved worldwide. www.zondervan.com The "NIV" and "New International Version" are trademarks registered in the United States Patent and Trademark Office by Biblica, Inc.™

All emphasis in Scripture quotations is the author's.

Cover design by Michael Dinsmore
Interior design by Dale Jimmo
Printed in the United States of America
28 27 26 25 24 23 22 21 20 19   1 2 3 4 5 6 7 8 9

To my children
Aiden, Leona, and David
May God fully conquer your hearts with His love.

Contents

Foreword	xiii
Introduction	1

Part 1: Discovering the Love of God
1.	It Takes God to Love God	7
2.	The Wrong Picture	17
3.	Defined by the Father	27
4.	The Father Revealed	37
5.	The Father's Affirmation	47

Part 2: Experiencing the Love of God
6.	Love's Beginning	59
7.	Love's Test	65
8.	Love's Assurance	75
9.	Loved in Weakness	83
10.	A Different Perspective	93

Part 3: Learning to Love
11.	Love, the Way of Holiness	107
12.	Loving Well	117
13.	Loving God	127

Acknowledgments	137
Notes	139

Foreword

What is the Spirit saying to the Church today? I believe that the thing the Holy Spirit is emphasizing the most is that He is establishing the first commandment in first place in His Church worldwide. Yes, Jesus is returning for a prepared Bride (Rev. 19:7).

The God who has everything is yet searching for something that He still wants first and most from His people. What does God search for? What does He want most and first? It is love that He is after. He is after our heart.

There is no agenda more central to the Father's heart than releasing grace to the human heart to glorify Jesus, by empowering His people to love His Son passionately and wholeheartedly (Jn. 17:26). Therefore, there is a corresponding need for every single one of us to receive grace from the Father for confidence in love that enables us to draw near to Him—empowering Christians to run *to* God rather than *from* God when they stumble.

Christianity is an ongoing encounter of love with a Person. Possessing fierce dedication and making radical choices for righteousness will not keep us steady unless we encounter the love the Holy Spirit pours into our heart (Rom. 5:5). It is not enough to be a part of a mission or have vision to change a city or nation. The labor of the vision will make us emotionally weary without the small but consistent stirring of love in our emotions by the Spirit. Stirred emotions in love are the most powerful force in the universe!

There are questions that arise from these ideas that become some of the most critical issues of our life and destiny. Who are we to God? How does He feel about us, even in our weakness and brokenness? Do we have a great and glorious future with Him and in Him, even after we stumble?

The title of Daniel Hoogteijling's new book, *Loved: When the One Who Knows You the Best Loves You the Most*, encapsulates one of the most powerful truths of the gospel and the greatness of God. The full and free acceptance, mercy, and incomparable loving-kindness we receive from Jesus at the new birth are among the most glorious things that have ever happened to any of us. Many Christians have difficulty believing that what we have received from God is real and true and personal. But when revelation of His acceptance produces security in our hearts, we will allow God to come as close as He wants. And that is closer than we think.

Daniel and his wife, Marlies, have boldly proclaimed this message for many years among our young people at the International House of Prayer of Kansas City. Under their excellent leadership, many young lives were transformed. I am so thankful for the fruit of their ministry and how they carry the heart of the Father. Daniel has been a trustworthy guide for many into these critical truths. I trust that, as you read, he can serve the same role in your life. May your heart connect to God in a transforming way; may He root and ground you in His unfathomable love—there is no greater reward for the man or woman who loves Jesus.

Mike Bickle
International House of Prayer of Kansas City

Introduction

You've been told that God loves the whole world, and that is true. But how does He feel about you personally? When you picture God looking at you, what is the expression on His face?

If you were at the right place at the right time, you could have heard Jesus praying on the evening of His arrest. Before His Father, He poured out His heart, saying, "'Father, I desire that they also whom You gave Me may be with Me where I am'" (Jn. 17:24). This is the heart's cry of a passionate God who longs for the nearness of His children.

After Adam and Eve had sinned, as they were hiding in shame, God asked the first question recorded in Scripture, "'Where are you?'" (Gen. 3:9). That same question echoes down through the ages because God wants us near, not in hiding.

Many believers, however, don't live in nearness to God. Instead, they live with hearts distanced by fear and shame. They may remember the initial revelation of God's love when they got saved. Their hearts were set free, and they felt so alive and loved! But those days might be long gone.

So often, we show up in church, but we're not really there. We try to be good because we know we should be. We keep ourselves busy but feel as if we are constantly falling short. Yet, deep down there is a desperation for real friendship with God. That desperation doesn't go away. We have tasted something, and we know we'll never be satisfied without it. We were made for the adventure of living in intimate fellowship with God, for a heart alive and free in the confidence of His pleasure over us. He made us to know and experience His emotions, to feel that He still likes us.

So easily our vision of God gets blurred by wrong beliefs about Him. Our life experiences want to tell us God can't be trusted. Nearness to God, then, seems elusive, the call to holiness an impossible demand and constant source of condemnation. We live more aware of our history of failure and current weakness than in awe of God's goodness and love. And it wears us out!

Paul the apostle prayed fervently for the Ephesians—a church community he loved dearly—that they would know the incredible scope of God's love and that they would be rooted and grounded in it (see Eph. 3:17–18). If we are not rooted and grounded in God's love, we reduce Christianity to a religious system in which there is no personal relationship, and we are left with some sort of sin management program.

However, God is deeply emotional and has powerful feelings toward His people. When the Holy Spirit connects our hearts to the pleasure in God's heart toward us, it changes everything. The fire of God's love revives our human hearts.

In 1871, just after the great Chicago fire had burned down one-third of his hometown of Chicago, the American evangelist D. L. Moody went to New York to raise funds for rebuilding the churches. Moody had been gripped for months with a hunger for more of God, and had been "'crying all the time that God would fill me with His Spirit.'"[1] Finally, while walking in New York, he had "'such an experience of His love that I had to ask Him to stay His hand.'"[2]

As Winkie Pratney relates, "After this baptism in the Holy Spirit, [Moody] began powerful evangelistic meetings with Ira D. Sankey, whom he had met the year before."³ Moody himself said, "The sermons were not different; I did not present any new truths; and yet hundreds were converted. I would not now be placed back where I was before that blessed experience if you should give me all the world."⁴

Of the famous Welsh revivalist, Evan Roberts, it was said that "wherever he went, hearts were set aflame with the love of God."⁵

Imagine the Holy Spirit setting your heart aflame with the love of God like never before. How would you live if you felt God loved you deeply and enjoyed you every day? Probably differently.

God wants you living fascinated in the revelation of who He is, confidently enjoying intimacy with Him as His beloved child. He wants to fully conquer your heart with His love.

Brennan Manning wrote, "How glorious the splendor of a human heart which trusts that it is loved!"⁶ God wants you to live in that reality. Let me help take you there.

To begin, let's rediscover the love of God—to know what His love for you looks like. When you truly start believing that the One who knows you the best loves you the most (and likes you, too!), you will be amazed at how enjoyable it becomes to relate to Him. When this love becomes real and personal, it changes everything. The greatest result of an increased revelation of God's emotions toward you is that your heart will grow in love for God.

In part 2, I want to compare your experience with God's love with the experiences of two individuals in the Bible. How God truly sees you in your weakest and messiest moments may be very different than what you have thought.

Lastly, in part 3, you will find that love is the way of wholehearted devotion. And so you will end your journey in this book learning how to love God and others well—all because of your confidence in God's love for you.

Part 1

Discovering the Love of God

1

It Takes God to Love God

In the second chapter of the book of Revelation, we find a message from Jesus for the Christians living in a place called Ephesus. This was a real, historical church in what is now modern-day Turkey. In the first seven verses, we find a personalized message from God to them. It is quite interesting. God tells them, "I know your works. I know all about you," and He then compliments them for the good they've done (see Rev. 2:2).

Apparently, the Ephesians were a hardworking bunch of people. They had labored for the Lord's sake. They had persevered through difficult circumstances, stuck together, and kept going (v. 3). They were committed to sound doctrine. They discerned when some false apostles came by, who were teaching weird stuff, and resisted their false teaching. God loved it and honored them for it. But then He said there was one thing He had against them (v. 4).

First Love Lost

One of the first times I studied this passage, I remember thinking,

If God had only one thing He was upset with me about, that would be pretty good! The problem with the church at Ephesus, though, was that the one thing they weren't doing was the most important thing—and that, of course, made all the difference!

These guys had lost their first love. They didn't love God the way they had at the beginning. The passion, the spiritual excitement in their hearts over the person of Jesus Christ had been slowly but surely fading. God got pretty intense with them real fast because this was not a side issue with Him. In fact, He told them to look at the height from which they had fallen (v. 5). And when He then told them to repent, He meant business. After all, loving Him was the main point, right? It was Commandment Number One.

In Matthew 22:37–38, Jesus said: "'"You shall love the LORD your God with all your heart, with all your soul, and with all your mind." This is the first and great commandment.'" The highest priority, the most important thing, according to Jesus, is that we love God with all we are and all we have.

Apparently, love for God can grow or fade as we learned from the situation with the church of Ephesus. You can cultivate it or move away from it, away from loving God the way you did when you first fell in love with Him. But this doesn't happen overnight. You gradually move away from your first love through the lifestyle you choose to develop. Slowly, your heart may grow cold while you maintain the outward appearance of being a wholehearted Christian. You may still go through the motions, but the desires of your heart have shifted. But you won't be happy settling for a mere outward appearance of being a Christian.

Why?

Because you were created to live with a heart on fire—a fire lit by the very fire that burns in God's heart!

I really love God's message to the believers at Ephesus, but at the same time, it scares me, because it teaches me that it's possible for a church to be committed to sound doctrine, to be evangelistically active, to be involved with many good activities, programs, and preaching—all the while deficient in spiritual passion, in fiery love for God. If it's possible for a church, then it's possible for a single individual like you or me to memorize a bunch of Bible verses, go on mission trips, help out with kids' church, share our faith with others, come to all the meetings, be there for years and years, maybe even have a reputation as someone who is faithful and perseverant, yet lack that spiritual passion, that excitement about the Lord Jesus inside the heart.

That, my friend, is a problem, because then we are missing the main point of life—to love God. R. A. Torrey, speaking of the command to love God with all our heart and soul and might, said, "the violation of the first and greatest of the commandments must be the greatest sin."[1]

Called to Love

When we find ourselves lacking spiritual passion, when we've moved far away from our first love, I imagine the Lord would then say the same thing to us that He said to the believers at Ephesus: "Look at the height from which you've fallen. Come back to Me" (see Rev. 2:5).

You can set your love on what you choose. You can direct your love. It's within your power. When you discover you are no longer loving God with the same zeal, you can do something about it. You can determine to make loving God the primary pursuit of your life. As Mike Bickle has said, "One of the most important decisions in our Christian life is when we intentionally determine that the 'primary dream' of our life is to live in the first commandment."[2]

In Psalm 91, God described some of the blessings experienced by the person who has "set his love upon" Him—blessings like protection, deliverance, and honor. King David was such a person. He was determined to love God. He wrote: "I will love You, O Lord, my strength" (Ps. 18:1). And God has called you to make loving Him the primary pursuit—the highest priority—of your life.

Your calling in life has a lot more to do with *who you are supposed to be* than *what you are supposed to do*. You are called to be a lover of God. That is the main reason you are on the earth. Of course, we partner with God in building His kingdom. We all have our assignments. But our primary calling has mostly to do with the size of our hearts, not the size of our ministries.

In John 17:26, Jesus prayed to His Father and said, "'I have declared to them Your name, and will declare it, that the love with which You loved Me may be in them, and I in them.'" This is so awesome. Jesus declared to His disciples the Father's name, meaning He showed the disciples what the Father was like. And the reason He did so was because He wanted the love of the Father to be in them—that His disciples would love Him as the Father in heaven loved Him. In fact, Jesus loved His disciples in the same way the Father loved Him. He said, "'As the Father loved Me, I also have loved you; abide in My love'" (Jn. 15:9).

His desire is that we do the same—that you and I would love Him in the same way the Father loves Him. Jesus wants to be loved by you and me. He wants us to abide in His love, and He wants to be known.

In John 6:2, we read that many people followed Jesus "because they saw His signs which He performed on those who were diseased." In verse 26 of that same chapter, we find Jesus addressing the people. He said, "'You seek Me, not because you saw the signs, but because you ate of the loaves and were filled.'" Jesus had just fed the five thousand men the day before. Many people followed Him for the miracles and the provision. And Jesus loved healing and delivering people and providing for them, for sure. Yet, at the same time, He looked for people who would follow Him for who He was, not just what He could do for them. He wanted to be known *and* believed. He then told people that He was the Bread of Life and that their fulfillment was found in knowing Him, a fulfillment that went deeper than what physical food could provide (v. 35).

Earlier, in John 5:39, Jesus had told those gathered around Him, "'You search the Scriptures, for in them you think you have eternal life; and these are they which testify of Me.'" In essence, Jesus was saying life is not found in just knowing the words of Scripture; knowing the Scripture leads to a real Person. We search the Scriptures to find the Person. And knowing Him causes us to come to life on the inside.

Since I'm from the Netherlands, I can tell you that the Dutch king, Willem-Alexander, was born in a city called Utrecht on April 27, 1967. I can also tell you he represents the Kingdom of the Netherlands, he married a woman from Argentina, and he has three daughters. Furthermore, I know that he knows how to fly a plane, how to snow ski, and how to ice skate. Lastly, I know where he lives, what he looks like, and what his favorite soccer team is. But I do not know *him*. I know about him, but I have no relationship with him. Additionally, I don't know what King Willem-Alexander thinks, what annoys him, what moves him, what friendship with him is like, what his dreams are for the future, or what his fears are.

In a similar way, God can be that familiar stranger—someone we know stuff about but not someone we know personally. J. I. Packer said, "A little knowledge *of* God is worth more than a great deal of knowledge *about* him."³ And he was right.

Jesus asked his closest friends, "'Who do you say that I am?'" (Mt. 16:15). And He asks you today, "Do you really know who I am?"

In Revelation 3:20, Jesus said, "'Behold, I stand at the door and knock. If anyone hears My voice and opens the door, I will come in to him and dine with him, and he with Me.'" This verse is often quoted in the context of evangelism. Frequently, non-Christians are told that Jesus is standing outside and "poor" Jesus is cold and wants to come in, so do Him a favor and repeat the prayer. But that's not how we should view this scripture. Revelation 3:20 was written to believers, people who were already saved. And God was basically saying, "Listen to Me. I want to come real close and fellowship with you. I don't want to be a familiar stranger. You were created to enjoy personal and intimate friendship with Me. You were called to love."

Love Returned

As a young teenager, I remember being in church on a Sunday morning, casually singing along during worship, when all of a sudden I had this awareness of what I was actually singing. I can't remember the song, but it had the phrase, "Jesus, I love You," in it. As I sang that phrase, I started to wonder whether I did love Him. It made me question myself, *Can I sing this song truthfully?*

Immediately, I stopped singing. After all, I had once heard someone say, "God could condemn the whole Church to hell for the lies it sings on Sunday mornings." So, I figured it would be best not to give God another reason to consider doing that.

After church, I walked home and was thinking about this: *Do I love Jesus?* Somehow that question had grabbed hold of me, and all day I was disturbed by it. I knew I was supposed to love Him, but I just couldn't figure out if I did. I grew up in a solid Christian home and knew about Jesus, but was there genuine love for God inside me? I wasn't sure.

That night, when I went to bed, I grabbed my Bible to read my daily bit of Scripture before sleeping and decided this time to read the story of the crucifixion from the moment Jesus was arrested to the moment He arose. It was a story I was familiar with, but this time it moved me more than usual. As I was reading, it struck me that His best friends left Him. I also seemed to realize a bit deeper how much He suffered physically. And that it was personal. All He went through was for *me*. He found *me* worth dying for. As I was lying there, I started to feel tears burning in my eyes. Then—and this may sound weird, but it was real to me—it was as if Jesus appeared in my room and stood by my bed. Not that I physically saw Him, but I knew that I knew that He was there with me.

An overwhelming sense of His presence came over me. And He spoke and said, "Daniel, I love you." At that moment, it was as if nothing else existed apart from Him. He could not have said anything more profound to me. His words pierced right into my heart. God Himself, who I had read about only a few minutes before, was there with me and spoke to me. He knew my name, and He loved me!

The tears were really rolling upon that realization, yet at the same time, I felt such a deep joy that a part of me wanted to laugh, so it became this strange mix of emotions. Soon, I started saying, "I love You. I love You, Lord. I love You." Next, I remembered the question I had been wrestling with all day—whether I truly loved God—and there I was with the words flowing out of me. It felt so natural to tell Jesus I loved Him. At that moment, the Bible verse in 1 John 4:19 came to mind, where it says we "love Him because He first loved us."

That night, God gave me a personal revelation of Jesus' love for me, and it filled my heart with love, causing me to tell Him over and over again that I loved Him. I learned that it takes God to love God. We can't make ourselves love Him. We can't simply set our hearts on fire with love for the Lord Jesus. We can't work it up. As we're told in Romans 5:5, "The love of God has been poured out in our hearts by the Holy Spirit who was given to us."

The love of God and the grace to love Him back are gifts from God. The Holy Spirit pours them out in our hearts because cultivating love for God is the primary emphasis of the Holy Spirit's work in our hearts.

Yes, we were designed to receive and respond to love. When we receive revelation of God's love for us, it fills our hearts with a love with which we can love Him back. We can love God when we first believe and experience His love for us.

We grow in love when we grow in the revelation of God's love. Our hearts become more passionate for Jesus when we gain greater revelation of Him and His passion toward us.

Since that night I experienced His love, I have never wondered again whether I loved Jesus, because I have never doubted His love for me. I had never before found something so exciting and so fulfilling. I couldn't help myself. I was hooked.

Experiencing Jesus' love in such a personal and extravagant way changed my whole religious experience. At first, being a Christian was about what I was supposed to do or not do, but then God became a real person, and being a Christian became about getting to know Him personally.

At the beginning, I didn't like going to church, standing in neatly organized rows, and singing songs for thirty minutes on Sunday mornings. But then worship became real to me, for I came to understand I was singing to a real Person. Worship became a fitting response to the revelation of who He is. There is a real Person there on the other end receiving my worship.

Friendship with God became meaningful to me as well. And it's so exciting! Andrew Murray (1828–1917), a pastor and author from South Africa, wrote something that resonates with me, "May not a single moment of my life be spent outside the light, love, joy of God's presence. And not a moment without the entire surrender of myself as a vessel for Him to fill full of His Spirit and His love."⁴

Because Jesus loved me so much, I wanted to live my life well in response to it. I wanted to love Him well. I decided to pursue a life of deep friendship with God.

Even though I still had much to learn, as a few years went by, I started to lose the excitement over Jesus' love. Because instead of living in response to God's free and unconditional love, I became more and more focused on trying to earn it. Much of that had to do with the wrong picture I had of God the Father.

Going Deeper

1. Do you remember the moment that you first experienced God's love for you personally? How did that impact your life?
2. Was there a time in your life that you loved God more than now? Do you remember what your life looked like in those days? And do you remember what your relationship with God was like?
3. Do you feel like you can honestly tell God that you love Him?
4. Would you live differently if you made growing in love for God the primary goal of your life?

Meditation Verses

Revelation 2:1–7
1 John 4:19
Matthew 22:37–38

2

The Wrong Picture

Several years ago, a few friends and I decided to memorize the entire book of Ephesians. My main motivation was to impress people. I thought it would be pretty cool to tell people I memorized an entire book of the Bible. I went for it.

Trying hard to memorize the first chapter and wanting to be the first among my friends to get this book down, I read through it over and over. I even wrote it out and recited it, doing whatever I could to make it stick. But it got hard very quickly as four of the first verses in the book are actually one *long* sentence! It says:

> Blessed be the God and Father of our Lord Jesus Christ, who has blessed us with every spiritual blessing in the heavenly places in Christ, just as He chose us in Him before the foundation of the world, that we should be holy and without blame before Him in love, having predestined us to adoption as sons by Jesus Christ to Himself, according to the good pleasure of His will, to the praise of the glory of

His grace, by which He made us accepted in the Beloved. (Eph. 1:3–6)

As I went over these verses again and again, something good happened. This passage suddenly came alive in me. Although my motivation had been terrible up to that point, God used the words I was memorizing to speak to me.

During that time in my life, I had tried to figure out who I was. Of course, I knew what my name was, who my parents were, where I was from, and what I was doing. I knew all kinds of things about myself, but I was wondering, *What is the deepest thing about me? What defines me more than anything else? Who am I really at the center, at the core of myself?*

As I was wrestling with these questions, I went through Ephesians 3:5 over and over again. God the Father "predestined us to adoption," the verse says—meaning He destined us for a particular purpose, and that purpose is adoption. It says, "by Jesus Christ to Himself, according to the good pleasure of His will." What became so clear to me was that the Father adopted me, through Jesus Christ, to Himself. And I thought, *That's probably the most important thing about me—I am God's child.*

Today, I know being God's child matters more to me than anything else that's true about me. Answering the question, "What is a Christian?" the theologian J. I. Packer said, "The richest answer I know is that a Christian is one who has God as Father."[1]

David Pawson, a Bible teacher from England, tells this great story of adoption that I really love.[2] It's about a friend of his from the north of England. This man was in charge of a "Borstal" institution, which was a type of youth detention center or a reform school set up for young people who had committed serious crimes. One boy in this school was particularly difficult. The man in charge couldn't do anything with the boy. He tried giving the boy the bread-and-water treatment, but that didn't work. Then, he gave the boy special privileges, thinking a more congenial approach might work, but the boy didn't respond positively to that approach either. The child was a rebellious kid, and nothing changed him.

One day, the man called this young boy into his office and told him, "Look, I've tried everything to get you turned around, but it's not working. I have one more idea, but I can't do it without your permission." He continued, "I want to adopt you. I want you to be my son, and I will be your father. You will bear my name. And if you get in trouble, from now on, it will be my name you drag down. But I want to bring you out of this place and have you come and live in my home."

Surprised by the offer, the boy said, "Yes."

As Pawson tells it, "If I told you that from that day the boy lived a perfectly good life, I'd be telling you a lie. But from that moment he *wanted* to," and therein lies the difference.³

I love this story, and something about it probably resonates within you as it did within me—most likely because to some degree it's our story. We were captive in our sin, wasting away our potential. And then God chose and pursued us. He said, "I want you to be My child. I want to be your Father. I want you to bear My name, and I will love you as I love My Son Jesus."

We accepted His offer, and God adopted us into His family. We now belong to Him. We are connected, accepted, and loved by a perfect Father who knows us and deeply cares about us. This is an awesome truth. But the sad thing is so many believers do not live in the reality of that truth. Even though they are Christians, their hearts are disconnected experientially from the reality of a Father in heaven who deeply loves them, whose heart is to care and provide for them, and who welcomes and enjoys their nearness.

My Own Disconnection

I was like that. I had the hardest time connecting with God the Father. Of course, I knew I was saved and a child of God, but in my everyday life, that was more technical information than a living experience. I came to realize this when God started speaking to me about it while I was living in Kenya, East Africa.

My wife, Marlies, and I lived in Kenya for eight years. We're both from the Netherlands. In fact, we grew up there. For years, we had dreamed of moving to Africa, however. Then, in our early twenties, we moved to Kenya to be missionaries. We settled in a town called Kitale, a mostly agricultural town in Western Kenya, and we loved being there.

One of the first things we noticed in our new hometown was the large number of kids who lived on the streets. We found them in every town in Kenya, but Kitale had a larger number than most. Many people simply referred to the street boys as the "glue boys" because they sniffed glue to get high.

Whenever we would go into town, we would always see these children. And, of course, they would notice us. To them, we were new, rich, white people. They would run up to us, each hold out a hand, ask for money or food, and look at us with their big, beautiful, hopeful eyes.

These children were suffering. Most of them were orphaned. Many were AIDS orphans. With both parents having died because of AIDS, these kids ended up trying to survive on the streets. They were so young and typically didn't survive too far into their teenage years. Few made it into their twenties or beyond. Sniffing glue, fighting diseases, ganging up together, stealing, and begging, they tried to survive as best they could.

Many people despised and rejected them, and they were often mistreated by people in authority. It was a hard life for the boys but even worse for the girls. The girls got abused, ended up pregnant, and sought abortions, often dying with their child. The kids went hungry too often and didn't receive basic medical treatment. We would see them regularly walking around with wounds on their feet.

When we moved to Kitale and came face to face with these kids, our hearts were moved as we began to realize what hard lives they lived. Consequently, anytime we saw them, we would try to reach out to them in some small way. We would buy them some food or pray with them. Marlies especially pursued some of them, trying to get to know them, but it was difficult. They weren't that interested in building relationships with us.

But then, after a year or two of living there, my attitude toward these kids changed. Where at first I felt compassion for them, more and more I started to get annoyed by them. And, I have to admit, they were a little annoying. We could not move about throughout the town without being approached by them and their demands. Whenever I was in town, they would always come to me begging, and if I didn't give them something, they would yell at me. And if I did give them something, it was never enough.

One time, Marlies and I had some visitors from the Netherlands. One of the ladies was walking in town with us when one of the boys touched her inappropriately. Another time before this, these boys had yelled bad things at Marlies. Uninterested in building a relationship with us, they only looked to us for food or money. As a result, I grew to think they were annoying, selfish kids.

One day, I drove to town to buy some groceries. As I parked my car in front of the supermarket, taking the key out of the ignition, I turned to the door to open it, and I saw three little kids running toward me. In my heart, I thought, *Here we go again.* I got out of the car when all three of them were there, each holding up one hand while hiding a glue bottle with their other and begging for money. As I looked into one of these kids' eyes, in that moment, God spoke to me. He said so clearly, "Daniel, the very characteristics in them that annoy you dwell in your own heart also."

That was shocking to me. I didn't even know what that meant. I ignored the kids, went into the supermarket, grabbed my groceries, and wondered what God's words to me were all about. The whole experience was disturbing. I thought indignantly, *I'm nothing like those kids.* After all, they were probably not even Christians. And I saw myself as a holy missionary, trying hard to behave and make God look good.

Back at home I went straight to my office to pray and ask God what He was saying. I knew He had spoken, but I still didn't understand what He meant.

After a few minutes of prayer, suddenly, I had an experience. I saw a vision, and in it I was standing outside in a wide, open space. It was winter as I saw snow on the ground, and it was getting dark. Standing there all alone, I felt cold when I spotted a little house somewhere far away in front of me. I could see smoke coming from the chimney, so I ran toward this house.

Arriving at the house and looking at the windows, I noticed there were no curtains, and with the lights on, I could look right into the house. I came up to a window, and I saw the family room of the house. An old man sat in a big chair in the room. He had two kids on his lap, one on each knee, and he was reading them a book. A few other kids were sitting around listening to the man read the story. Then I was startled as two kids ran right by the window I was looking through. One of them had a bow and arrow and was chasing the other. As my eyes continued to scan across the room, I noticed some other kids playing with a train set on the floor. It seemed like there were kids everywhere! All of them appeared to be happy in the presence of this father figure. There was a sense of safety, of peace, and of warmth.

I remember that all I wanted in that moment was to be inside in the presence of that father and be like one of those kids. But I was on the outside looking in. And then the vision stopped.

Sitting there in my office and thinking about the scenes from my vision, I heard God start to speak to me. And I began to see how this vision described my experience in relating to God as Father. I felt like I had no connection to Him, as if I didn't know Him. I didn't feel loved by my Father in heaven. I felt as if I didn't belong but was on the outside looking in.

THE WRONG PICTURE

I knew I loved Jesus and felt deeply loved by Him. His death on the cross was incredibly meaningful to me. He loved me to the point of death and was my best friend. And I also loved the Holy Spirit. He was a real Person to me. I knew Him; fellowship with Him was real; and He was my best friend who was always there. But the Father—I could not relate to God as a Father. In fact, honestly, I was scared of Him.

If you would have asked me then what God was like, I wouldn't have described Him as I will now, but emotionally I related to the Father as if He were a really, really old man with long, grey hair. He wasn't seated on His throne, in my mind's eye, but He was standing behind the balcony of heaven with a baseball bat behind His back and looking down at me over His reading glasses. I thought He was a grumpy, demanding perfectionist who was always watching me, ready to pounce on me when I did something wrong.

I imagined God swinging His bat and rolling His eyes, disappointed that I couldn't get my act together. I imagined God saying, "Daniel, I knew you were weak, but I didn't expect this. Go pray and fast for a few days, and then come back and check in with Me again."

There was a part of me that always felt like I was letting God down. The way I thought about my salvation experience was not helpful either. I grew up in a good Christian home. My parents and family were mostly all believers and great people whom I loved. They were all going to heaven. And I wanted to go there, too. I had learned about hell. I don't even like really hot weather, so I was convinced hell was not going to be a good fit. Plus, I figured I didn't want to be on the losing team.

I imagined trying to get into heaven, seeing myself carefully opening its door, peeking in, and seeing God seated on a massive throne with Jesus next to Him. Everything there was clean, white and gold and holy and pure. And there were angels, and it was all beautiful in my imagination. But then there was this dirty, little sinner named Daniel who was trying to get in. That's how I pictured myself. As soon as I stepped foot into heaven, I could hear an alarm going off, and the speaker system warning, "Contamination! Contamination!" Of course, God saw me. And God doesn't tolerate sin and wants to keep heaven clean. So, I imagined the Father saying with a loud voice, *"No!"* as He stretched out His hand toward me with lightning flashing from His fingers sent to pulverize me.

Thankfully, Jesus was seated next to Him, and Jesus loved me and wanted to save my life. Jesus in that moment jumped up and ran toward me, and then the scene moved into slow motion as Jesus dove in front of me and the lightning struck Him in the chest. Jesus then fell dead to the ground right in front of me. Everyone in heaven saw it and went quiet. My heart raced as I looked to the Father. He looked at me and looked at His Son who had just died in my place, and then looking back at me again, He said, "Well, I guess that just happened. Daniel, you're in. Go find a place here in heaven. Don't call Me. I'll call you if I need you."

That's how I imagined I got saved. You can understand why God was scary to me. I saw Him as the God who wanted to kill me but technically couldn't anymore because Jesus came between us. I was so thankful for Jesus but scared of God the Father.

My name, Daniel, means "God is my judge." That just made me nervous.

Growing up, my family had this candy jar at home, and the rule was that each of us kids could have two pieces of candy per day. One day, when it was just my mother and me at home, she said, "Daniel, I need to run an errand and will leave you here at home." She proceeded to remind me of the two-candy rule and said, "Remember, even though no one is here, God sees everything." This was supposed to serve as motivation—to keep me from stealing candy. But because of my flawed picture of God, it only confirmed the idea I had that God was always looking at me just to check whether I was doing something wrong.

My relationship with God felt more like that of a policeman and a criminal than a father and a son. Though I felt deeply loved by

Jesus, I didn't feel loved by God the Father. I felt merely tolerated by Him.

I heard a missionary tell of a dream she had in which God the Father organized a big banquet and invited all His children to come, eat, and fellowship with Him. She saw a huge table with all the finest foods on it. And then a little rat sneaked into the room, climbed up on the table, grabbed a grape, and scurried off. She woke up from the dream, and God told her that was how so many of His children feel—like dirty rats in His presence. When I heard her recount her dream, I felt exposed because that was exactly how I felt—unworthy to draw near.

My best friend had a very different experience. He had been to a conference that was all about the love of the Father. He really connected with God as his Father during that season of his life. And he kept saying, "God loves you. You've got to experience His embrace. Just sit on your Abba-Papa-Daddy's lap and let Him hold you."

I couldn't relate to that. God was not like that to me. My God was a consuming fire. If I were to sit on His lap, I'd burn my behind! Besides, He was my judge; I mean, who snuggles with a judge?

As I was sitting in my office, God showed me that I was indeed very much like those orphaned street children in Kitale. They didn't have a home. With no father to care for them, they had to live in their own strength, striving and trying hard to survive. I began to see I was living as if I didn't have a Father in heaven who loved me and cared for me. I lived as if I had to survive in my own strength, always trying to impress God and earn a place in His heart. I was selfish, and my world revolved around what I could and should do to gather for myself what I needed to survive.

I realized I had a problem.

Going Deeper

1. What is a good definition of a Christian?
2. If you had to describe what your heavenly Father is like, how would you describe Him?
3. When you honestly reflect on your relationship with God the Father, do you feel like you know Him?
4. If you imagine the Father looking at you, what do you see in His eyes?

Meditation Verses:

Ephesians 1:3–6
1 John 3:1–2
1 John 4:18

3

Defined by the Father

When we have a wrong picture of what God is actually like, our ability to relate to Him will be hindered. Our hearts will shut down toward Him. We could sing along in church but have a heart withdrawn from Him because deep down we are afraid of Him, afraid He will reject us, or <u>afraid</u> <u>He is disappointed in us</u>. I am not talking about a healthy, biblical fear of God based on who He truly is, but I am referring to a "scaredness" based on a <u>false picture</u> of who God is and what He is like.

Brennan Manning, in his book called *Abba's Child,* tells a story of a friend who has a handicapped son. The son's name was Daniel. The son reminded me of myself.

> One night [the father] asked his handicapped son, "Daniel, when you see Jesus looking at you, what do you see in His eyes?"
>
> After a pause, the boy replied, "His eyes are filled with tears, Dad."
>
> "Why, Dan?"

An even longer pause. "Because He is sad."

"And why is He sad?"

Daniel stared at the floor. When at last he looked up, his eyes glistened with tears. "Because I'm afraid."[1]

If you don't have a revelation of God's love for you personally, you will strive to earn His love. Because we were made for His love, it is the only thing that will truly satisfy us.

Spiritual Orphans

Many Christians, dearly loved by the Father, live as spiritual orphans. They live as if they don't have a Father who loves and cares for them. They don't know the place of rest in the unconditional love of their Maker. Because they don't expect anything good to come their way from the Father, they have to make it happen in their own strength. Life then becomes all about what they can do. This makes for a very tiring life of constant striving.

When Jesus came to the earth, He came to fix the separation. "I will not leave you orphans," He said. "I will come to you" (see Jn. 14:18). He didn't want us to live with our hearts disconnected from the Father.

Jack Frost wrote,

> If you (or a church) have an orphan spirit, as I did for a long time, you feel as though you don't belong. Love, value, honor, and acceptance are foreign concepts to you. You believe you have to act right, dress right, talk right, and do right in order to be loved and accepted; and even then, it still doesn't happen. You feel as if there is something more you have to do or put in order to find rest and feel valued. With a spirit of sonship, however, you feel loved, valued, honored, and accepted for who you are as God's creation. You have no need to "prove" yourself to anyone. As a son or daughter, you feel a sense of total love and acceptance. Contrarily, as an orphan, you feel like you are on

the outside looking in, trying as hard as you can to perform and be good enough to earn a place in someone's heart.²

As I said in chapter 2, that is exactly how I felt. That is what I saw in my vision. I felt like I was on the outside looking in.

To some degree, we are all familiar with this. Only Adam and Eve experienced a perfect connectedness to God—until they sinned. They chose to turn from God and go their own way. Their sin broke the heart connection between them and God. All following generations know and experience the separation.

Something in us all wants to go our own way. We have inherited an independent spirit. We don't want to submit to God; we want to be our own god.

Something in us wants us to make a name for ourselves. We want to accomplish things in our own strength. If we want to experience intimacy with God, however, we have to turn from this independent attitude.

Jesus is a great example for us. He was a perfect Son who lived for and drew life from His relationship with His Father. He surrendered His will, saying not His will but the Father's will be done (Lk. 22:42). He spoke the words of His Father and did what He saw His Father doing (Jn. 5:19; 12:49). Often withdrawing in prayer, clearly He lived intimately with His Father who was in heaven.

A heart humbly submitted to the Father comes to life. Like Jesus, the children of God acknowledge where they came from and submit to their Father. Instead of seeking to make a name for themselves, they say, "Father, I give You the right to define me. I want to derive my sense of self-worth, my sense of identity, from You and You alone."

There are many things that are true about us, right? For me, it is true that I am from the Netherlands, that I am married and have lived in Kansas City, Missouri, and Kitale, Kenya, East Africa. I have three kids and a dog. I have certain strengths and weaknesses. I've done things well, and I've messed up. There are some people I know, and billions of people I don't know. And I love scuba diving, and I hate eating liver.

A lot of things are true about me. All those things together make up the story of my life.

The same holds true for you. There are many things true about you, good and bad, and they make up the story of your life. That's fine. The problem, though, is when we take something that is true about us and make that the truest thing or most important thing about us. If we then allow that to define us, we encounter problems.

Why?

Because everyone builds their identity around what they believe is the most important thing about them. So, when we overidentify with something that is true about us, it messes with our sense of identity.

For example, many people overidentify with what they do. They derive a sense of value from what they do. It gives them their sense of self-worth. Therefore, they conclude that they matter or have value because of what they do. But people can overidentify with other things—things like what they have, how they look, whom they know, whom they are dating, or what their position is.

As God's children, only one thing is *the* most important thing about us. It's the thing that should define us more than anything else. It's the deepest thing about us.

What is it?

It's that we are children of the Father who made us and loves us. It should be what matters most about us and what defines who we are more than anything else. It's the source of true self-worth and where we find our confidence. We don't overcome insecurities through achievement but through believing and experiencing how God feels about us.

People may also overidentify with things that are negative about themselves. They battle with a horrible sense of self-worth because they have allowed something negative that is true in their lives to define who they are. It can be something bad that happened to them, or it can be something bad that they have done. It could be a persistent sin that they are fighting. The devil loves it when we let our sin define us. But we are not our sin. You are not your sin. It is not the deepest thing about you.

The devil knows your name, but he calls you by your sin. God knows your sin, but He calls you by your name. *yes good*

When we look to something or someone to give us our sense of self-worth, we are also empowering that something or someone to take away our sense of self-worth. What if we lose our jobs, or our spouses leave us? Or we lose our possessions, or are not invited to sing on the worship team anymore?

Henri Nouwen said, "If you know you are Beloved of God, you can live with an enormous amount of success and an enormous amount of failure without losing your identity, because your identity is that you are the Beloved."[4]

David Lomas, in his book, *The Truest Thing About You*, also addresses the idea of overidentification. He asks a great question that helps us see where we stand with this. I'm phrasing it here in my own words: What is it in your life right now that is giving you your strongest dose of self-confidence?[5] Think about that for a minute. What is your primary source of self-worth right now?

God wants to be that.

For years, I lived by a very unhealthy formula. I believed that my accomplishments plus people's opinions of me equaled my importance as a person. When I was achieving good things and others spoke highly of me, then I felt valuable. I felt I had the right to sit "at their table," as it were. But that formula made me a slave to the opinions of others. Later on, that got exposed as I experienced times I had to work with individuals who didn't know me, especially when I had to come alongside leaders whom I respected. At those times, when I felt insecure, I still tried to prove myself with my good works because my confidence was built on my ability to impress others. I had to repent of this.

Don't do what I did. Don't look to people or things to define your worth. I had to turn away from listening to people's opinions and turn to the Father. I had to ask forgiveness for looking to people to validate me when the Father wanted to do that. I had to stop striving and stop trying to make a name for myself. Instead, I had to allow God to name me. Instead of trying to create self-worth, I had to discover it in God.

Identity Secured

When an inventor creates some sort of new machine that supposedly is going to change our lives, the day comes when he presents it to the world. He organizes a big unveiling. People pack the room, the inventor pulls the sheets off this machine, the music plays, and confetti and balloons falls from the sky as he tells everyone what it is that he has built. Because he has built it, he has the power to name it, right? After all, it is his invention. And if it were to break, he would be the only one who could fix it, because he knows what it is and how it is supposed to work.

God made you. He invented you. He knit you together in your mother's womb (Ps. 139:13). You were made on purpose. There are accidental parents, but there is no such thing as an accidental child. Because He made you, only He has the right to name you, to define you. No one else has the right to assign value to you or declare your worth. And when you break, God can fix you. He knows what you were made for and how you are supposed to work.

We can't earn an identity; it can only be given. The Father is the one who gives identity to His children. So, I had to submit to the Father and give Him permission to be my source of confidence. As the apostle Paul said, I had to "bow my knees to the Father of our Lord Jesus Christ, from whom the whole family in heaven and earth is named" (Eph. 3:14–15).

God loves it when His children come to Him and allow Him to define them. He loves it when we stop our striving and humbly submit to His declaration of worth over our lives.

Jesus' disciple John is a great example of someone who found his sense of value in God's opinion of him. John, like us all, had to learn to find his identity in God and not in what he did, what he had, or what other people thought of him. On a few occasions in John's gospel, we read the identity John discovered in Christ as seen in his references to himself: "Then Peter, turning around, saw the disciple whom Jesus loved . . . who also had leaned on His breast at the supper" (Jn. 21:20). John wrote his gospel when he was an old man. What's amazing is that John referred to himself as the disciple "whom Jesus loved" (also in John 13:23).

I believe that is the primary way John viewed himself. His referring to himself that way shows us what was most important to him. John was the one who was loved by God. And, of course, he was. Jesus loved John in the same way that the Father had loved Him (Jn. 15:9).

When Jesus and the disciples had the Last Supper together, John was the one who had been right next to Jesus, leaning on His chest. What a very intimate picture this is of his relationship to Jesus. John wanted to be as close to Jesus as he could be.

It's important to note, however, John was far from being a perfect disciple. None of Jesus' disciples were. Earlier, Jesus had rebuked John as he and the others had been arguing over who was the greatest among them. But there was no shame in John. His immaturity and failures didn't keep him from seeking to be as close to Jesus as he could be.

There was John, leaning on Jesus, resting in His presence. As imperfect as he was, John was at peace in the presence of a perfect God before whom all his sins and immaturity were an open book. Jesus knew everything about John. There was nothing hidden, yet John felt secure in Jesus' love. Because John understood that the One who knew him the best also loved him the most.

This makes me think of the story in the Old Testament about a man named Mephibosheth. He was Jonathan's son and King Saul's grandson. His father was King David's best friend. In the biblical narrative, we read that Mephibosheth was a five-year-old boy when his father and grandfather died in battle, after which David became the new king of Israel. It was custom among some in those days, when a ruler was defeated, for all his family to be killed to rule out the possibility of someone from the previous king's lineage trying to reclaim the throne. So when the boy's caretaker heard that both the boy's father and grandfather had died in battle, she took Mephibosheth and fled with him, endeavoring to protect him from his assumed fate. She succeeded in hiding him, but in her haste the boy fell and became lame in both feet. Born to royalty, he remained hidden as he grew up with no inheritance, in poverty, and in a desolate place called Lo Debar.

Then one day, King David asked, "'Is there still anyone who is left of the house of Saul, that I may show him kindness for Jonathan's sake?'" (2 Sam. 9:1).

A servant who had worked for King Saul informed David that Mephibosheth was still alive. David sent for him, and he was brought before the king. Fearing for his life, Mephibosheth fell to his face, prostrating himself. King David then gave him the best news he had heard in all his life:

> "Do not fear, for I will surely show you kindness for Jonathan your father's sake, and will restore to you all the land of Saul your grandfather; and you shall eat bread at my table continually." (2 Sam. 9:7)

Mephibosheth couldn't believe what he was hearing, so he said in response, "'What is your servant, that you should look upon such a dead dog as I?'" (2 Sam. 9:8).

What a sad response. Clearly, Mephibosheth didn't think very highly of himself. And I can understand it. He was a descendant from the previous king, and he had nothing to offer David. He was a poor, lame man who was of no benefit to David's kingdom. David didn't even know him. He was an insignificant nobody. Yet, he received from King David the privileges worthy of the son of a king.

The story ends with this statement: "So Mephibosheth dwelt in Jerusalem, for he ate continually at the king's table. And he was lame in both his feet" (2 Sam. 9:13). This is so awesome! Despite Mephibosheth's shortcomings, he sat at the highest place of privilege—at the king's table.

Mephibosheth's story raises this question: How can someone sit at the king's table despite his being cripple? We ask ourselves similar questions like, "How can I be in with God despite my sinfulness? How can I get God to love me despite my weakness? How can He use me when I have nothing to offer?" And the answer to all those questions is one word: *grace*. We sit at the table, not because of what we have done, but because of who Jesus is and what He has done.

How could John the disciple, as imperfect as he was, sit completely at rest in the presence of a perfect God? Because Jesus loved John and John had boldness in His love. Neither Mephibosheth nor John had earned their respective places at the table. They were undeserving. But they were not unworthy. There is a difference.

You see, we are undeserving of God's love but not unworthy in His eyes. Jesus found us worth dying for. You and I are accepted, not only despite what we have done, but also because of who we are. You are dearly loved by God. He made you and, according to God, everyone has inherent value. You're not valuable because of your skills or skin color or social status. Your value is not assigned to you for any reason. Your value is inherent.

When we look at the life of the disciple whom Jesus loved, we find that John held on to that identity or revelation for the rest of his life. It was the banner over his life. John became quite an accomplished leader in the church. He was a revival leader, planted churches all over Asia, wrote several books of the Bible, and was a friend of other famous church leaders. His name was written on the foundation of heaven for all of eternity. And when Jesus died, He entrusted His mother—the person who was probably dearer to Him than anyone on the earth—to John's care. Now, that is impressive!

In all the books John wrote that are in the Bible, he made no reference to his own name. Of all the titles he could use to identify himself, he chose the one that truly defined who he was. He was the disciple whom Jesus loved. Think about that for a minute. That was how John wanted to be known—as the one loved by God. Let this give you a vision for your life—to be defined by God's love and to derive your sense of value from it.

When we find our identity in God, we stop trying to become who we think we should be and simply become who we are. We move from fantasizing about who we want to be to living in the glorious reality of who we are, dearly loved children of God.

Going Deeper

1. What do you think is the most important thing about you?
2. What in your life is giving you your strongest dose of self-confidence?
3. How does (lack of) awareness of God's love influence how you live?
4. What if you could have a meal with Jesus and sit next to Him? How would you feel; do you think you'd be comfortable in His presence?

Meditation Verses:

Psalm 139:13–14
Ephesians 3:14–15
John 13:23

4

The Father Revealed

I understand that we can't just change our feelings about God, but we can change our thinking. I have found that our feelings typically follow our thinking. When we have wrong beliefs about God, they will give us emotional hindrances in relating to Him. If we think rightly about God, we will end up feeling rightly about Him.

Romans 12:2 talks about transformation that comes to us when our minds are renewed. To change our thinking, our minds need a good reset. And to enjoy intimacy with God, we must displace the lies in our thinking with the truth of who God is and what He is like. The truth about God is found in His Word. Giving His Word was actually God's invitation to us to get to know Him. He wants us to know Him.

John addressed children in 1 John 2:13 when he said, "I write to you, little children, because you have known the Father." He revealed a wonderful truth in this verse, that God the Father can be known—and not just by smart theologians. No, John said children can know God the Father, which means you and I can know the

Father. It is our joy and privilege to get to do so and draw closer and closer in a deeply personal relationship.

Here are some key truths about the Father that He wants you to know—truths that will change how you see Him.

The Father Sent the Lord Jesus

First, the Father sent the Lord Jesus. I know this is really basic, but it is important. As I said in chapter 3, I had this idea that God wanted to kill me but technically couldn't anymore because Jesus rescued me. That made me thankful for Jesus and left me scared of the Father. But those were emotions rooted in false beliefs.

First John 4:14 tells us, "And we have seen and testify that the Father has sent the Son as Savior of the world." John 3:16 says, "For God so loved the world that He gave His only begotten Son, that whoever believes in Him should not perish but have everlasting life.'" These two verses confirm the truth that the Father sent the Son for our salvation.

My concept of God wanting to kill me and Jesus preventing Him from doing so was not true. The Father was the one who sent Jesus because the Father loved me and wanted to save me.

The whole plan of salvation was the Father's idea. He made a way for us to be reconciled to Himself without violating His holiness and His justice. And He did this because He wanted to. Ephesians 1:3–5 declares, "Blessed be the God and Father of our Lord Jesus Christ, who has . . . predestined us to adoption as sons by Jesus Christ to Himself, according to the good pleasure of His will."

The Father made it possible through Jesus to adopt us to Himself. Scripture tells us that is how He wanted it, and that is what gave Him pleasure. You and I were wanted and pursued by the Father who bought us, paying the highest price.

Jesus Came and Revealed the Father to Us

Jesus knew the Father intimately. He came from the very bosom of His Father and revealed to us the truth concerning Him. John 1:18 tells us, "The only begotten Son, who is in the bosom of the Father, He has declared Him."

Jesus taught us about His Father so that we also could know the Father's love. We read in John 17:26, when Jesus was talking to His Father, that He said, "'I have declared to them Your name, and will declare it, that the love with which You loved Me may be in them, and I in them.'" Sent by His Father, Jesus came to the earth to reveal to us what the Father was like, to show us the love He shares with the Father, and to love us with that same love He shares with the Father. Think about that for a minute.

Philip, one of the disciples, wanted to know the Father. He actually wanted to see the Father, so he approached Jesus and said: "'Lord, show us the Father, and it is sufficient for us'" (Jn. 14:8). And Jesus answered him, "'He who has seen Me has seen the Father'" (Jn. 14:9).

Hebrews 1:2–3 tells us that Jesus is the express image, or you could say, the exact representation of the Father. The apostle Paul understood that truth. He told the Corinthians that Jesus is the "image of God" (2 Cor. 4:4). What does all this mean?

It means Jesus said what the Father said, did what the Father did, and loved as the Father loved—all as the exact representation, the express image, of the Father. The very love of the Father was shown to us through Jesus. And nothing, "neither death nor life, nor angels nor principalities nor powers, nor things present nor things to come, nor height nor depth, nor any other created thing, shall be able to separate us from the love of God which is in Christ Jesus our Lord" (Rom. 8:38–39).

The love of God the Father was made visible primarily through the life and death of Jesus Christ. Jesus came, and He put the Father's love on display for all to see. When you consider Jesus' death on the cross, how He loved you to the point of death, know that is the love of the Father made visible to you. The love of God is in Christ Jesus.

Jesus taught His disciples about His Father. And He told them, "'The Father Himself loves you'" (Jn. 16:27). Jesus says the same to you today. He says, "Trust Me. I know Him, and He loves you!"

Jesus Came to Reconcile Us to the Father

Jesus not only came to show us what the Father was like, He also came to reconcile us to the Father. He didn't want to leave our hearts orphaned, disconnected from our heavenly Father, so He came to fix the relationship (see Jn. 14:18). He came to give us peace with God (Rom. 5:1). He came so that God would "'be a Father to you,'" and for you to be God's child (2 Cor. 6:18).

Jesus said something absolutely amazing! He said that He and the Father would come and make their home with us (see Jn. 14:23). Where was Jesus' home? Where did He come from? He came from the bosom of the Father, remember? He came from the right hand of the Father in heaven. He knew what it was like to lean on His Father's chest and find rest in the rich love and safety of His Father. That is where Jesus came from, and that is where He returned: "'I came forth from the Father and have come into the world. Again, I leave the world and go to the Father'" (Jn. 16:28).

Jesus is saying, "What the Father and I have, that intimacy together in heaven, that fellowship, I want you to enter into that. What the Father and I share, our home, we're going to bring that reality into you." Now, that is amazing!

Jesus actually asked, "'Father, I desire that they also whom You gave Me may be with Me where I am'" (Jn. 17:24). He desires for you to be with Him in the presence of the Father. Allow me to say this another way: Jesus wants you there with Him *and* the Father. Jesus' sacrifice on the cross made it possible to enter into a deeply personal relationship with God the Father that, one day, will result in your dwelling in the Father's house for eternity!

We Can Come Near as His Beloved Children

The apostle John, excited and amazed by our new life in God, proclaimed, "Behold what manner of love the Father has bestowed on us, that we should be called children of God!" (1 Jn. 3:1). We are God's kids!

Can you believe how much God loves us? What a privileged position is ours. "In Christ Jesus [we] who once were far off have been brought near by the blood of Christ" (Eph. 2:13). And because we are His beloved children, through Christ, we have direct access "by one Spirit to the Father" (Eph. 2:18). Here we have the entire Trinity in one verse—through Jesus, by the Holy Spirit, to the Father!

Not only do we have direct access to the Father, but also now "we have boldness . . . with confidence through faith in Him" (Eph. 3:12). The writer of Hebrews said we have the kind of boldness necessary "to enter the Holiest by the blood of Jesus," permitting us to "draw near with a true heart in full assurance of faith" (Heb. 10:19, 22). Our boldness before God is rooted in what Jesus has done for us. We don't relate to God on the basis of our own righteousness. No, Jesus made us righteous.

We don't have to earn our way into heaven. Through Jesus we were born into God's family. It brings glory to Jesus' work on the cross when we enjoy intimacy with God the Father.

Today, we can "come boldly to the throne of grace, that we may obtain mercy and find grace to help in time of need" (Heb. 4:16). When is our time of need?

Often, our time of need is when we would naturally feel the least bold—when we are battling temptation or when we have messed up. Surprisingly, that's exactly when God says, "Come to Me now." He is not intimidated by our messes and our messiness. If we have a wrong picture of God and mess up, we will run away from Him in fear instead of toward Him. But He beckons us to come to the throne of grace. The apostle James tells us to "draw near to God and He will draw near" to us (Jas. 4:8). And when we come to the Father, He doesn't reject us. He responds with love.

The Holy Spirit Makes Us Experience the Reality of Sonship

Romans 8:15–16 says we have "received the Spirit of adoption by whom we cry out, 'Abba, Father.' The Spirit Himself bears witness with our spirit that we are the children of God." The Holy Spirit of adoption makes us experience the reality of this. The Spirit bears witness in our hearts that God is our Father. *Abba* is a Hebrew term that essentially means *Daddy*. It is an affectionate term that children use to address or refer to their father who loves them and provides safety for them.

In Galatians 4:6–7, Paul expressed the same idea a little differently. He said, "And because you are sons, God has sent forth the Spirit of His Son into your hearts, crying out, 'Abba, Father!' Therefore you are no longer a slave but a son, and if a son, then an heir of God through Christ."

God freed us to live as sons and daughters. We are not slaves; we're sons and daughters! And then the Father sent the Holy Spirit who pours the Father's love into our hearts: "The love of God has been poured out in our hearts by the Holy Spirit who was given to us" (Rom. 5:5).

One of my all-time favorite Bible verses, which also gives me a vision for something I want to do at the end of my life, is 1 John 1:3. It says, "Truly our fellowship is with the Father and with His Son Jesus Christ." John, that disciple whom Jesus loved, wrote this when he was an old man. He was in the later stages of his life, and I love this statement that he made. When I am old and about to check out of life on this earth, I want to gather together all my kids and their spouses and their kids and their kids—however far down the generations go—in my living room. (They can even bring their pets.) And then, I want to testify of this great truth, telling my family that, truly, we have fellowship with God the Father and His Son.

THE FATHER REVEALED

Christianity is not a system of rules to manage behavior, it is not merely historical, and it is not simply about a book. Christianity is real fellowship with God Himself. It's a personal relationship with the Creator of the universe. And He is not a distant God. He can be known. He is not an elusive, hidden, grumpy, old perfectionist. True, He is holy and all-powerful, but He is also good, innocent, pure, kind, and loving. He is a Father who loves to relate to us and wants us to draw near in confidence and talk with Him.

What God the Father Thinks of You

Some two thousand years ago, there was a bold prophet living in the wilderness of Judea called John the Baptist. For hundreds of years, God had been silent. God's people were waiting for promises to be fulfilled. When John showed up with a message from God, hope was stirred. Could it be that God was visiting His people again?

All over the land, people were talking about John. Thousands of people would walk for hours into the wilderness just to hear him. There was something different about him. When John spoke, he did so with unusual authority on his lips.

Imagine you were there, standing among the crowd along the riverbank, watching and listening to John call people to repent from their sins—seeing him baptize them. At one point, perhaps, a Man waded into the water and asked to be baptized. Could you imagine John looking at Him and saying, "No, Lord, I need to be baptized by You"?

John baptized the Son of God, and you just witnessed it. You saw Jesus come up out of the water, and with water dripping from His body, He prayed. And when He prayed, the heavens opened above Him, and a dove descended upon His shoulder. What an incredible scene, but that wasn't all. You heard a voice. And it wasn't just any voice. It was the voice of the Father declaring over His Son, "'This is My beloved Son, in whom I am well pleased'" (Mt. 3:17).

Powerful! The Father said, "He belongs to Me. He is My Son.

And I am pleased with Him." These are the words that all of humanity desperately longs for. These are the words that satisfy the deepest human need for love and acceptance.

Now, of course, it makes sense that the Father would be pleased with Jesus, because He was perfect. Jesus obviously was the ideal Son. I am not.

When I was fourteen years old, I got baptized in my home church. I had to wear a strange white robe over my clothes, and after I was dunked underwater, the worship team led the church in the song I had requested. And so, it happened. I came up from under the water, and the song started to play. I stood there wet and looked around. No dove showed up. Or maybe it was outside looking for a way to get in? I don't think the heavens opened up either, and I didn't hear the Father in heaven thundering down a powerful declaration over me, saying that He was proud of me. I've wondered what He was thinking, though, when I got baptized. Surely, He saw me at least.

Could it be that what the Father said to Jesus is the same thing He says to us? Could it be that what He declared over His Son Jesus is the declaration He makes over you and me?

When Jesus died on the cross in our place, He offered us a great exchange: His innocence for our sins. When you are born again by repenting of your sin and accepting and trusting in what Jesus did for you, then you are made clean. You receive the innocence of Jesus Christ. And just as Jesus stood in the Jordan River that day, clean, you stand before God today, clean, as clean as Jesus.

The Bible also teaches us that the Father loves us as He loves His Son Jesus. He has no favorites. And we know that He never changes. God the Father, the unchanging Creator of the universe, loves you as He loves His Son Jesus.

This is the great truth: what the Father said to Jesus *is* the same thing He declares over your life. Charles Spurgeon said, "Do you not realize that the love the Father bestowed on the perfect Christ He now bestows on you?"[1] And I want you to receive that.

Forget about what other people have said about you. Forget about how you feel about yourself. Humbly submit to God's Word. Submit to the Father, and let Him define you. Only He has the right to do so. Your Father in heaven says to you, "You are My son." He says, "You are My daughter." He thunders, "I am proud to be your Father, and I love who you are. You bring joy to My heart."

And you just have to believe this—whether you feel it or not. Feeling it won't make it true. It already is true. Some charismatics have the idea that something is only real if you feel it. But when you are waiting to feel something instead of simply believing it, you are running around a truth in circles. And you'll never own it.

I don't think it is wrong to seek to experience God's love. That is yours to know as His child. Seeking the experience can be done in a right way or in a wrong way, a way that will actually keep you at a distance from His love. I believe it is faith that makes the difference.

We can come with a childlike expectancy, with faith in who God is, or we can come with unbelief. When we are seeking an experience in order to believe, that's called *unbelief*. We're essentially saying, "God, prove to me that what You say is true by letting me feel it." If that's how you approach Him, then you will relate to God as if His love for you is not true until you feel it. And then you are placing feelings above the truth declared in God's Word.

Don't do that. It's time to change your mind. It's time to have a change of heart, too. Receive the words from His Word. Agree with what God's Word says is true regardless of your feelings today. That way you posture your heart to experience the reality of the Father's love and stop circling around it.

Going Deeper

1. Are there things you think about the Father that are actually not true?
2. What are some Bible verses that teach you something about what the Father is really like?
3. With Jesus being the express image of the Father, what do you love about Jesus, and what does that tell you about what God the Father is like?
4. Even if you don't feel lovable, can you now make a choice to just believe God loves you because that is what is true?

Meditation Verses:

John 3:16
John 16:27
Matthew 3:17

5

The Father's Affirmation

Imagine meeting my wife and asking her, "Does Daniel love you?" and hearing her respond, "Hmm, wait a minute. You know, that is a good question! Let me think about that. I'm not sure. I hope so. We've been married for a long time, and he is still here. I guess that is good, right? I sure love him and want him to love me. Did he tell you he loves me?"

If that were her response, it would be horrible! I would hate to hear that Marlies questioned my love, because I love her. I wouldn't want that to be something my wife wondered about, something she questioned. I would want her to know that she has a husband who deeply loves her. I would want my kids to know the same, that they are greatly loved by their dad. If you asked them if I loved them, I would hate to hear them answer, "Maybe. Sometimes. When we behave. We hope so, anyway."

If I, an imperfect husband and father, want my wife and children to know I love them, how much more does our Father in heaven want us to know He loves us? He doesn't want it to be a question we are wrestling with. He wants it settled in our hearts, where we know that we know our Father in heaven loves us profoundly.

The Father doesn't want you to strive in attempts to earn His love. He wants you to sleep in the peace of knowing that you're in, that there's nothing you have to do to earn His acceptance or affection. God loves you now. He is not waiting for an improved version of you. He is not waiting for you to mature. He loves you now, not later when you have it all sorted out.

You are fully known and completely loved. He enjoys you with the knowledge of your sins and with the knowledge of your weaknesses. And even in your immaturity, you bring Him great pleasure.

God's love for you is unconditional. That means that it doesn't depend on what you have done or will do or are currently doing. His love for you depends on who He is. And God is love. He has always loved you. There has never been a day in your life that you were not loved. He put you together in your mother's womb and has loved you all the days of your life. The good days. And all the bad days.

The Nature of His Love

I love my wife, but I also love my kids. Not only do I want them to know I love them, I also want them to really know that God loves them—always. So, at times, I'll ask my kids, "When does Jesus love you?"

And they will answer, "Always."

Then I'll ask them if He loves them when they are in school, when they are sleeping, when they are bored, or when they are playing. I like doing this to keep them aware of the Father's love.

On one night in particular, I was putting my kids to bed, and I was sitting on the side of my five-year-old daughter's bed. I asked her, "When does God love you?"

"Always," she replied.

Then, I decided to ask some harder questions. She and her

brother had had a fight earlier that day, so I asked her, "Does God love you when you bite your brother?"

"Yes," she said without any hesitation.

"Yes, He does still love you. What about when you are in the bathroom?"

She laughed a little. It seemed inappropriate, but her reply was the same, "Yes."

"And what about when you don't listen to your father?"

"Yes."

"Really? Do you think God loves you when you are not listening to your father?"

"Yes," she said, smiling broadly.

"You're right. He does, but you still have to listen, though!" And then I asked a question I had not asked her before: "But Leona, why does God love you?"

She answered immediately with a roll of her eyes and flick of her head back like a model, "Because I am so beautiful."

I loved it—and said to my daughter, "Yes, Leona, you are very beautiful. God made you this way because He wanted you this way." Of course, God loves her not just for her looks, but I thought it was a win for her at that point to be confident that she is a beautiful creation designed by her heavenly Father and that God loves her.

Shortly after that, I picked up my two eldest kids from school. My son was sitting in front with me, and Leona was in the back seat. As we were driving home, I said, "Aiden and Leona, I love you."

Without missing a beat, Leona, as she kept looking out the window, muttered, "Yeah, I also love myself."

Aiden and I had to laugh about it, but at the same time I thought, *What a great response!*

Sometimes, I wish I could love myself a little better. I have met so many people who look in the mirror every day and hate what they see. I don't know what you see when you look into the mirror. Chances are you don't see yourself as God sees you. What do you think God sees when He looks at you? How does He feel when you come to mind?

I remember my eldest son did something wrong and felt very guilty about it. He hated that he had sinned. He wanted to hit or somehow punish himself. He had the hardest time forgiving himself and moving on. I remember holding him and talking to him. I wished he could have seen himself as I saw him. I wished in that moment he could have felt how deeply I loved him in spite of what he had done.

Sometimes, God just wants to hold His children even as they are squirming in shame and hating who they are. In such times, He simply asks them to believe in His love for who they are despite what they have done.

He Sees You

Leona is my little princess. There are times I ask her why she is a princess, and she answers, "Because my Father is the King." And that's right. Her Father in heaven is the greatest King of all kings, and she is His daughter. That's pretty special.

Leona really got into those Disney princess characters. She even had several princess dolls. She loved them because they were so beautiful to her. One day, she came to an important realization: princesses wear dresses. Suddenly, she saw it. Every one of her princess dolls wore a dress. And in the movies, they all wore dresses as well. Leona then decided that, since she was a princess, she should also wear dresses—and only dresses—because there was no princess who walked around in pants. Her wardrobe, however, contained both dresses and pants. If she waited for her mommy to come and dress her in the morning, then there was about a fifty-fifty chance she would have to wear pants. And that was a risk she could no longer take.

For several weeks, as soon as she woke up, Leona got out of bed and grabbed a dress out of her closet. She would work her little body

THE FATHER'S AFFIRMATION

into it, which was challenging at times because most of her dresses had some closing mechanism in the back. That meant her brother had to help. Once princess Leona was dressed in her dress, she would go downstairs and look for me to present herself. She would come up to me and show off her pretty dress, twirling around in front of me and looking at me.

Every morning, she put on her show. And even though she never articulated it, I always felt like she was asking me two questions. The first one was, "Daddy, do you see me?" And the second one was, "Am I beautiful to you?" In other words, "Do you like what you see?"

Somehow realizing the importance of the moment, I made sure to drop whatever I was doing and look at her twirling in her dress. Sometimes, I would tell her, "Leona, I see you." I would say each time, "Leona, you are so beautiful. I can't believe it. Please twirl again." And she would twirl and make her dress flare. Occasionally, she would fall over and have to get back up again, fixing her dress and twirling some more with a big smile on her face, until her heart was full and princess Leona was ready for her day. The next morning, she would do it all over again.

I wonder if there is something in a woman's heart that, like a little girl, wants to ask her Father in heaven the very same questions. Perhaps there is something in you that wants to come before the Father and ask Him, "Do You see me? Have You noticed me? I am sure You see the pastor's wife or maybe someone like Joyce Meyer, but have I caught Your eye also?"

And then the big question, "Do You like what You see? Am I beautiful to You?"

I want you to know the Father says to you, "Yes, My daughter, My eye is on you. And I love what I see. You are beautiful to Me."

I don't know how God did it, but He put something inside each one of us that makes Him look at us again and again. God made us to be unique. There is no one else like you. There is no one else like me. We know that, but what it means for you is that you move the heart of God like no one else can.

Sometimes, we get so down on ourselves and wonder whether there is any reason to live. *What difference would it make if I checked out of my relationship with God or out of life?* But it would make a great difference. You can never be replaced. If you quit, God will never have something that only you can give Him. The relationship you and God have, as weak as it may seem today, no one else has.

My daughter needs the affirmation of her father, but my sons need it as well. This is not girlie stuff. Jesus, the most powerful and courageous Man in the world, needed to hear the Father declare His love over Him. Men need to hear the voice of their Father in heaven speaking affirmation over them. If God's love is not real to men, it leaves an emptiness that nothing can satisfy. For some reason, we men have this tendency to look to women for what we have not found in God. No woman can give us what only God offers.

The Nature of Your Father

One night, when I was three years old, my father, who was sleeping in the room next to me, died in his sleep. My parents were missionaries, and we were living in the Middle East at that time. This was devastating. My mother moved us back to the Netherlands, and later she remarried. Growing up with my natural father absent was an experience I projected onto God. I expected Him to be absent. I lived as if He were in heaven with my natural father, totally disengaged and uninvolved with my life down here on the earth. Our picture of God is often greatly influenced by our life's experiences.

I don't know what your experience has been, but I know there are no perfect fathers. In fact, many people have had fathers or father figures in life who greatly misrepresented God the Father.

Maybe your earthly father was absent. Maybe he was there but never affirmed you, leaving you to feel as if you were never good enough. Now you live before God the Father, and you are still trying to prove you are good enough. You are still trying to earn a father's approval.

The Christian life, though, is not about what *you can do* to make yourself worthy of your heavenly Father's acceptance. The Christian life is about trusting in what *Jesus did* to make you worthy of His acceptance.

God is not like your earthly father. He is a perfect Father. We've got to see past our man-made image of God and recognize Him for who He really is.

When Jesus hung on the cross, we could barely recognize Him physically because of what people had done to Him. In the same way today, we must look past the hypocrisy and the failures of sinful men and see that God is still God. And that God is still good. Nahum 1:7 tells us so: "The Lord is good." God really is good. He always is good.

I heard a story years ago that I have never forgotten.[1] There was a woman who was still living with her family. They lived in a big city in a Muslim country. The whole family was Muslim, but the young woman encountered Jesus and secretly became a believer.

One evening, her father found out that his daughter was secretly a Christian, and he got really angry. He started to beat his daughter, and then disowned her, saying, "You brought shame upon my family—shame on you!"

Then, the father stripped her naked and physically kicked her out of the house and onto the street. She started running down the street, crying in her nakedness. She realized she needed help and knocked on a door. A family took her in, and it turned out to be a Christian family.

A few weeks later as she was walking somewhere in town, she was recognized by someone. The woman came up to her and asked, "Hey, what were you doing a few weeks ago running down your street so late at night? Where were you going, and why were you wearing that beautiful white dress?"

Apparently, God covered her nakedness so that she appeared clothed to this woman. That is what our Father is like. He covers our shame.

Some time ago, a friend and I went to teach at a Bible school. I did the first class, and after a little break, she did the second session. I sat in the back with the students and listened to her excellent teaching. At the end of the class, she said to the students, "Let's do a little exercise. I want everyone to close their eyes and ask God a question."

I liked what she was asking us to do. I was ready for a good learning exercise.

The students and I started closing our eyes while she continued giving instructions, "Ask God, if He wanted to play a game with you, what game it would be."

My eyes flew open. I didn't like what she asked us to do. It just felt very uncomfortable to me. I didn't want to do it. I take God very seriously. I don't play games with Him, and I didn't want to start. However, I didn't want to interrupt the exercise, so I just sat there quietly. I didn't ask God the question. I was very skeptical, I might add, of the endeavor.

After a while, some of the students who participated in the exercise started to cry softly. I wondered what was up. Maybe they didn't like the game, or maybe they played and lost? Maybe God rebuked them for asking that question? I didn't know quite what to think.

A few moments later, my friend closed the prayer time and asked if any of the students wanted to share what God had spoken to them. I sat back and listened, still a bit skeptical of it all, when one of the students who was in tears said she wanted to share what God had done.

"A few years ago, my sister became very sick and was hospitalized. I would visit her every day after school, and we would play this board game together," she began to tell us. "We both loved it. One day, I got a call from the hospital. My sister had died," she continued in tears. "I decided I would never play that game again. I was in so much pain, and I couldn't make sense of her death. Offended with God, I buried the pain and tried to move on with my life. This morning, when I asked God what game He'd like to play with me, He asked if I would play the board game I used to play with my sister with Him."

God was asking the student if she would let Him come to the most painful part of her past. She said *yes* that day, and God started healing her.

Will you trust your heavenly Father and believe in His love? He wants you to know His love. He wants you to know that He is good.

Thank God, you are not fatherless. You have a good Father.

Going Deeper

1. Do you find it hard to love yourself? Why? Do you think those reasons make it hard for God to love you?
2. How do you think your experiences with your earthly father have influenced your idea of what God is like?
3. Is there an area of immaturity in your life where you need the Father? What would you long for Him to do or say?

Meditation Verses:

Romans 8:38–39
Nahum 1:7
1 John 1:3

Part 2

Experiencing the Love of God

6

Love's Beginning

A great way to understand more of God's nature and how He relates to us is by looking at how He related to others in the Bible. Seeing the Lord's leadership, for example, in Peter's life reveals so much of God's nature and can cause our hearts to grow in confidence before God on both good and bad days. Then, there's the Shulamite woman in the Song of Songs. She fell in love with King Solomon. I see her relationship with the king as analogous to Peter's relational experiences with Jesus. Like Peter, she was confronted with her shortcomings and shame, and found freedom in grace and love. Taken together, their stories give us some beautiful insight into God's heart.

In this chapter, as well as chapters 7 and 8, I want to explore the relational experiences of Peter and the Shulamite, seeing how those experiences apply to our lives today. To do this, we'll lay Peter's, the Shulamite woman's, and our storylines next to each other to gain greater understanding of God and His love for us.

First, let's dive into Peter's story.

Peter's Beginning

Peter's story began when Jesus called Peter to follow Him:

And Jesus, walking by the Sea of Galilee, saw two brothers, Simon called Peter, and Andrew his brother, casting a net into the sea; for they were fishermen. Then He said to them, "Follow Me, and I will make you fishers of men." They immediately left their nets and followed Him. (Mt. 4:18–20)

I love this. Jesus found Peter, invited him to be His follower, and then immediately made a commitment to make something of the fisherman—to make him a fisher of men. And that is how it works. When God calls, He doesn't look for the qualified; God qualifies the willing. He looks for the willing, and then He says, "I will make something of you."

When we read the story of Jesus calling the disciples, Jesus almost seemed to call them randomly. But it wasn't random at all. The fact is Jesus talked to His Father all night before He chose the disciples. If I had been Jesus, I think I would have picked my disciples differently. I think I would have gone to the University of Jerusalem, talked to the head guy there, and explained to him that I was God and that I needed twelve disciples. I would have asked the head guy at the university for his best young men. I would have wanted strong, good-looking men who were fit because they would have to walk all over the place with me. I would have wanted men who were articulate because I would be leaving them with the most important message ever—a message that they would have to pass on to the world!

Jesus didn't seem to look for the best of the best. He looked for the quality of a willing heart. And Peter had that quality. That's why Jesus asked Peter to follow Him. Being willing, Peter immediately left everything and followed Jesus.

For the next three years, Peter and Jesus did life together. What a privilege for the fisherman. It is hard to imagine what it must have been like to spend three years with the Son of God. So many adventures. So many miracles.

To hear the Lord Jesus Himself preach must have been incredible. People were amazed by the gracious words that He spoke and by His wisdom and authority. Peter had a front-row seat all those years and could ask Jesus questions all day long.

Jesus and His disciples spent a lot of time hanging out together, eating, and talking about the kingdom. They laughed together, cried together, and witnessed powerful healings together, but they also saw the great need of the people who were lost without God.

Over those years, Jesus loved and invested much into His disciples. Jesus was a perfect Man, and He loved His disciples perfectly. This must have had an effect on Peter's heart. Peter grew in love for Jesus. In fact, Jesus became everything to him. Jesus became the Lord of Peter's life.

Just before Jesus' death on the cross, He shared a meal with His disciples and told them that one of them would betray Him. That was shocking to them, causing each one to ask Jesus, "Lord, is it I?" (see Mt. 26:22). John asked. James asked. Thomas asked. And Peter asked.

Then Jesus replied, "'He who dipped his hand with Me in the dish will betray Me'" (Mt. 26:23).

Judas looked at his fingers, and he knew who the betrayer was. Judas turned to Jesus and asked Him, "'Rabbi, is it I?'" (Mt. 26:25).

Jesus affirmed, "'You have said it'" (v. 25).

It is interesting to note that all the disciples referred to Jesus as *Lord* except for Judas. He called Jesus *Rabbi,* meaning teacher. The way we address God reveals what we believe about Him.

For the disciples, Jesus had become the Lord of their lives, but not for Judas. It was not uncommon in those days for teachers to have disciples who would follow them around for a season of training. To Judas, Jesus was a teacher—someone with interesting things to say, someone worth following around, but not someone who was the Lord of his life.

To Peter, Jesus had become everything. He had left everything to follow Jesus. He received the love of the Lord Jesus, and it caused Peter's heart to love the Lord Jesus in return. Up until that point, Peter was in a great place in life. He was enjoying friendship with Jesus, and the future was looking bright from his perspective.

Jesus was the promised Messiah who would bring the kingdom of God. He was prophesied to bring an end to all of Israel's enemies, and He would rule the world from Jerusalem. And Peter was right there with Him!

Let's leave Peter's story here for a moment and look at our other example.

The Shulamite's Beginning

In the Song of Songs, we discover a love story between King Solomon and a Shulamite woman. Solomon wrote this poetic book describing their relationship from its early beginnings to mature love in marriage. Primarily, the book contains the feelings and experiences expressed by Solomon and the woman. It begins with the Shulamite woman speaking:

> The song of songs, which is Solomon's.
> Let him kiss me with the kisses of his mouth—
> For your love is better than wine.
> Because of the fragrance of your good ointments,
> Your name is ointment poured forth;
> Therefore the virgins love you.
> Draw me away!
> We will run after you.
> The king has brought me into his chambers.
> We will be glad and rejoice in you.
> We will remember your love more than wine.
> Rightly do they love you. (Song 1:1–4)

Here is the beginning of their relationship. The Shulamite had fallen in love with King Solomon. All she wanted was to be with him. She wanted him to kiss her. She was ecstatic about his love, saying it was "better than wine." Hers was poetic language. Wine here represented the pleasure of the world. The woman was really telling the king that his love was better than anything else the world could offer her.

She was captivated by the king. She wanted him to draw her away. She wanted to do life with him. When she thought of the future, she imagined it with this man, this king.

Your Beginning

The Shulamite maiden experienced all the emotions of someone in love. You may have felt those same emotions at one point. They are powerful feelings. Maybe you know what it is like to fall in love. Your life could be a mess, but when you fall in love, everything changes, right? Suddenly, you are excited about the future. You dream about being with that other person. You start picturing yourself together with the one you love. He or she is all you can think about as you float around on cloud nine.

If you'll remember, Peter was in a similar place. He had fallen in love with Jesus. He had great hopes for the future, and all he wanted to do was spend the rest of his life with the one who loved him so well.

What about you? There was a time when you first met Jesus. You met a Person who was greater than life. And He offered you a love that was better than anything this world could offer. All you wanted was to love Him and be with Him and live for Him. Your heart was awakened to the reality of His presence and greatness. It was your first love.

Do you remember those early days of your relationship with God—the days when He conquered your heart? When He gave you a future and a hope? You decided to surrender to Him. You made Jesus Lord and dedicated your life to Him. You wanted to serve Him, to run with Him and follow Him wherever He would lead you. Those were happy days for you as they were happy days for Peter and the Shulamite in their stories.

      Peter   Shulamite   You
      ☺   ☺   ☺

Going Deeper

1. Think back on how immature you were when you first started following Jesus—did God love you even though you were so weak and immature?
2. Was there a time in your life when you were more captivated by God's love, less worried about your shortcomings, and more excited about the future than you are now?
3. If so, what changed?

Meditation Verses:

Matthew 4:18–20
Song of Songs 1:1–4

7

Love's Test

Peter, the Shulamite, and you were all in a happy place at the end of chapter 6. The beginning of love is something wonderful. But let's look at what happens next in your lives.

Peter

Peter was doing great, but he still had a lot of things to learn. Peter was a very confident disciple. Not that confidence is bad, but his was an immature overconfidence in his abilities and in his understanding. At one point, he even tried to correct Jesus (see Mk. 8:31–33). Jesus was talking about His upcoming death and resurrection, and Peter basically said, "Lord, You're wrong. That's not going to happen." Jesus then had to give Peter a pretty strong rebuke.

Jesus kept up the conversation, telling His disciples that He was going to die and informing them that He would rise again. In the final days of Jesus' life on the earth, He shared a last meal with His disciples. It's what we refer to as the Lord's Supper. At the end of the meal, He and the disciples sang a song together and went out to the Mount of Olives.

Then Jesus said to them, "All of you will be made to stumble because of Me this night, for it is written: 'I will strike the Shepherd, and the sheep will be scattered.' But after I have been raised, I will go before you to Galilee." (Mk. 14:27–28)

The disciples didn't want to hear that. And Peter couldn't believe that he would stumble and abandon Jesus. In his overconfidence, Peter responded, "'Even if all are made to stumble, yet I will not be'" (v. 29). It is almost funny. Peter thought himself different from everyone else, so self-assured.

Then Jesus spoke, "'Assuredly, I say to you that today, even this night, before the rooster crows twice, you will deny Me three times'" (v. 30).

Man! You would think those sobering words would quiet Peter, but no. Verse 31 tells us, "But [Peter] spoke more vehemently, 'If I have to die with You, I will not deny You!'"

Peter thought he knew better than Jesus. Peter was convinced he would be faithful even to the point of death. The other disciples seemed to draw courage from Peter's strong statements, and all agreed with him. They were sticking with Jesus.

What's interesting to note is it wasn't too long before this exchange that the disciples had been arguing over which of them was the greatest. We don't know how that conversation went, but I am pretty sure Peter was heavily involved in that discussion. I can just imagine him playing his walking-on-water card. It was King Solomon who, many years earlier, noted in the book of Proverbs that pride comes before a fall (16:18).

After the disciples argued, Jesus told Peter, "'Satan has asked for you, that he may sift you as wheat. But I have prayed for you, that your faith should not fail; and when you have returned to Me, strengthen your brethren'" (Lk. 22:31–32). Jesus knew Satan wanted to separate Peter from Himself. And Jesus knew the pride in Peter. Nothing was hidden from Jesus. He knew exactly what was going to happen.

What was Jesus' response?

LOVE'S TEST

Jesus prayed. He told Peter He prayed for him. Jesus expressed no rejection or anger at Peter. It's as if He said, "You are going to mess up, but I will not reject you. I am praying your faith won't fail. I want you to come back to Me and let Me use you to strengthen your brothers." Amazing!

Jesus knew exactly how weak Peter was, but He loved him nonetheless. In fact, Jesus knew Peter better than anyone else on earth ever would, including his family and closest friends. Yet, knowing Peter's pride, selfishness, and arrogance, Jesus actually loved Peter more than anyone else on earth ever would. He even continued to include Peter in His closest circle of friends.

Next, Jesus took His disciples into the garden of Gethsemane to pray. He wanted them to stand with Him. He took Peter, James, and John a little deeper into the garden and told them, "'My soul is exceedingly sorrowful, even to death. Stay here and watch'" (Mk. 14:34).

Jesus moved still farther away from them to be alone with the Father. Jesus was wrestling in prayer, surrendering to the will of the Father. This was a very intense moment in Jesus' life as He would soon be facing unimaginable hardship. Jesus was deeply distressed, and His closest friends—Peter, James, and John—kept falling asleep. Finally, Jesus told Peter (who was also called Simon), "'Simon, are you sleeping? Could you not watch one hour? Watch and pray, lest you enter into temptation. The spirit indeed is willing, but the flesh is weak'" (Mk. 14:37–38).

I'm not sure if Peter fully understood what Jesus was telling him. Peter may have thought, *Sure, I'm willing. I'll do whatever You want. My flesh weak? I'm not weak—I'm ready to fight for You. I'll die for You. I'm only a little tired today.* Soon, however, Peter would understand what Jesus said to him here.

We know what happened next. Jesus was arrested, and all the disciples fled. One after the other disappeared in the darkness of the night.

What about Peter?

Well, he didn't completely run away. Scripture says he left, but he followed Jesus from a safe distance (Mk. 14:54). That never works. There is no such a thing as following Jesus from a safe distance. A lot of people look for a middle road, endeavoring to balance selfish desires and comfortable loyalty to Jesus—giving up the things they don't mind getting rid of, yet not fully surrendering to Him. Jesus warns us about seeking a self-preserving life. He said, "'If anyone desires to come after Me, let him deny himself, and take up his cross, and follow Me'" (Mt. 16:24). Self-preservation will not work. You will be miserable. You were made to live all in.

It didn't go well for Peter. He betrayed the Lord Jesus. Lukewarm Christianity will lead you to the denial of Jesus Christ. You will end up giving up on God.

Three times, Peter denied Jesus that night. The third time Peter denied Jesus, a rooster crowed, and being within eyesight, Jesus at that moment looked Peter straight in the eyes (Lk. 22:61). Then Peter remembered Jesus' words, how Jesus had told him that, before the rooster crowed, he would deny Him three times.

Peter's world collapsed, and he went away weeping bitterly. This was such an intense moment in Peter's life. What he thought would never happen, did happen. What he thought he would never do, he did do.

I have often wondered what the expression on Jesus' face was as He looked at Peter. What did His face communicate as He looked Peter in the eyes? Was it a sad, disappointed look? Was it an "I-told-you-so" look? Was it an angry face?

No, I doubt Jesus' face communicated anger or condemnation. While we don't know for sure because it is not explicitly mentioned in Scripture, I think what shone from the face of Jesus communicated this: "Peter, I love you. I love you. I love you." Scripture tells us that it is God's kindness that leads us to repentance (Rom. 2:4).

When Peter looked into Jesus' eyes, he broke down and wept.

This was probably the lowest point of his life. He had betrayed Jesus. His whole world crashed. All his hopes and dreams were connected to this Man. Peter had left everything for Him. So, Peter thought it was all over and decided to go back to fishing. I wonder if the disciples were good fishermen. They never seemed to catch anything, but this was the old life that Peter knew.

After three years of incredible experiences with Jesus, suddenly, Peter was sitting in a little fishing boat in the middle of the lake. I can imagine him staring out over the water and feeling deeply ashamed. I'm sure he couldn't believe what had happened. The words of Jesus, "Your spirit is willing but your flesh is weak," probably echoed through Peter's head. It made sense to him then. He had blown it, and he felt utterly weak and defeated. Peter had wanted to be faithful to Jesus, but clearly his determination hadn't been enough to make it all work.

Peter	Shulamite	You
☹	☺	☺

The Shulamite

Let's go back to Song of Songs. That lady is still there, all giggly, happy, excited, and in love—thinking everything is perfect. Let's see how things develop for her.

The Shulamite woman in our story had fallen in love. And the first few verses of Song of Songs were filled with the excitement and optimism of that newfound love.

Soon, reality kicked in, and she realized that, just because she found love, not all was as it should be. In this part of the story she faced shame as she became aware of her own shortcomings:

> I am dark, but lovely,
> O daughters of Jerusalem,
> Like the tents of Kedar,

Like the curtains of Solomon.
Do not look upon me, because I am dark,
Because the sun has tanned me.
My mother's sons were angry with me;
They made me the keeper of vineyards,
But my own vineyard I have not kept.
Tell me, O you whom I love,
Where you feed your flock,
Where you make it rest at noon.
For why should I be as one who veils herself
By the flocks of your companions? (Song 1:5–7)

This comparison of the tents of Kedar with the curtains of Solomon actually highlighted a great contrast. The Kedarites were desert nomads. Their tents were made of black goatskins. Picture dusty, tanned, goatskins contrasted to the beautiful, clean, richly decorated curtains hanging in the holy place in Solomon's temple. Though she tries to believe she is still lovely, like Solomon's curtains, she immediately tells the king not to look at her. That's how negatively she saw herself.

The Shulamite didn't want the king to look upon her because her skin had been darkened by the sun. Being from the Netherlands—maybe because we don't get that much sun there—whenever the sun starts coming out after the winter, we roll up our sleeves and try to catch some sunshine. It is not cool if we are bright white, so we start working on our tans. But there in the Shulamite's country and time, it was different. White skin was viewed as being more desirable. It said something about your social and economic standing. Skin tanned by the sun was seen negatively as it was associated with the poor who had to work outside.

Something was different about her words at this juncture. In the first four verses of Song of Songs 1, the Shulamite was enraptured in her king—it was all about him. Starting in verse 5, however, something shifted. Her attention transferred from King Solomon to herself. And as she focused on her own being, she realized she was imperfect. She became aware of her shortcomings, and shame set in. The Shulamite didn't even want people to look at her lest they noticed her imperfection. Where at first she was captivated by the king's beauty and filled with hope for the future because of him, now her attention riveted on her deficiency. She knew she was at least lovely, but at this point she was seeing only her darkness.

The very next thing that happened with the Shulamite maiden was she lost sight of King Solomon. She then asked where he fed his flocks so she could find him.

The shift here is dramatic. The Shulamite went from being caught up in the beauty of the king to being stuck in shameful self-awareness and losing sight of the king. She was in a similar place to where we left Peter at the beginning of this chapter. In fact, her statement about being dark yet lovely resembles what Jesus told Peter in the garden before His arrest—about Peter's spirit being willing but his flesh weak.

The Shulamite and Peter felt alone and battled feelings of shame and failure. They were disappointed in themselves and missing the days of being with the one they loved—King Solomon for the Shulamite and King Jesus for Peter.

Peter	Shulamite	You
☹	☹	☺

The same thing happens in our lives. We get saved, the Lord touches our hearts, and we come alive. We feel the freedom of being loved as we are, and we look forward in hope to the future. Then, one morning, it's as if we wake up and don't feel like reading our Bible. We begin to look at ourselves instead of Him, and we realize that we are still imperfect. We still feel temptation. We make a mess of things. It's embarrassing. We do what we should no longer be doing. We find desires in us that we think should be gone—desires we act on, desires we yield to.

At times like these, the devil loves to come around and send you down the path of shame. He comes with accusation. He wants you to believe you are a terrible Christian, you are the only one who is this sinful, you are not where you should be, and God must be pretty disappointed in you. If the devil is successful, you start feeling like a failing Christian. You try harder, but it doesn't help. You keep falling short. And you experience the same shift in your attention as the Shulamite in our story. Where at first you were in love and captivated by God, now you look at yourself and are captured by your own sinfulness.

If you have a wrong picture of God, as we discussed in an earlier chapter, you will run from God instead of to Him when you mess up. You will withdraw and try to fix yourself and your problems.

God never withdraws from you; you are the one who runs away, afraid of His alleged rejection, because surely God couldn't put up with your brokenness. At least, that's what you think. And that's where many Christians live. We feel like we should be better. And, boy, do we try, but we can't ever be good enough. We feel like God is barely tolerating us but in no way enjoying us. If we are honest, we think He might even be mad at us and done with our inability to get our act together.

Restless and ashamed, you may know God forgives, but you feel badly that you are weak and failing so often. You still consider yourself a Christian, but your life certainly doesn't look victorious. Perhaps, initially, you thought you were radical in your relationship with the Father, but now you hope no one finds out what you are like in reality—who you really are.

If this goes on for too long, then the time comes when you give up. You disqualify yourself. You start thinking back to your old life. Remember, Peter went back to fishing. And when things got hard for the Israelites after their miraculous deliverance from slavery, they started thinking about the food in Egypt and wanted to go back. It was as if they had forgotten that life in Egypt was terrible!

LOVE'S TEST

You don't need the food of Egypt; you need an encounter with the heart of God in the midst of your brokenness. You need grace. At this point in the narratives, nobody is happy.

    Peter   Shulamite   You
    ☹   ☹   ☹

Going Deeper

1. Have there been moments in your life when you were really disappointed with yourself? Do you think God was surprised?
2. If God, who is good and safe, would take you aside and ask you what the areas of deepest shame in your life are—what would you tell Him? I encourage you to tell Him.
3. How does shame influence your relationship with God?
4. When you mess up, do you feel confident to approach God or would you rather hide?

Meditation Verses:

Hebrews 4:16
Song of Songs 1:5–6
Romans 8:1

8

Love's Assurance

Only a short while ago, Peter, the Shulamite, and you were happy. Then, certain events changed all of that. Your love was tested, and you thought your relationship changed—maybe even that your love was lost. But was it? Let's return to the three stories and see.

Peter

Peter was disgraced. Jesus was crucified and buried. Three days later, two women both named Mary and a woman called Salome went to the gravesite early in the morning. They went with spices to anoint Jesus' body.

When they arrived, they found the large stone blocking the entrance to the grave rolled away. They stepped inside. To their astonishment, they didn't see the body of their Lord. Instead, they saw an angel sitting where Jesus should have been at rest. Pretty spectacular! The angel calmed them down and then gave them a message from God:

You seek Jesus of Nazareth, who was crucified. He is risen! He is not here. See the place where they laid Him. But go, tell His disciples—and Peter—that He is going before you into Galilee; there you will see Him, as He said to you. (Mk. 16:6–7)

The three women stood there shaking and amazed as they listened to the angel.

This portion of Scripture is incredible. God sent an angel to go to the gravesite, sit there—waiting for the women to come—and then tell them that Jesus wanted to meet the disciples, *and Peter,* in Galilee! Peter was only one of the disciples, but the angel specifically mentioned him by name.

God was pursuing Peter, specifically calling him by name. How wonderful! God never gave up on Peter. Instead, He sought him out. What a picture of grace—love that searches us out when we have nothing to offer in return.

It's as if Jesus came to Peter, who was looking down in shame, and gently lifted up his chin and said, "Peter, look into My eyes; look at Me. I am not giving up on you, and I have something to say to you."

In John 21 we find Peter, back to his life of fishing, in a boat with some of the other disciples. They had been fishing all night but caught nothing. In the morning, however, they heard someone calling to them from the shore. It was Jesus! He told them to cast their net on the right side of the boat. They did what Jesus said and caught a multitude of fish.

Peter and these disciples recognized Jesus, pulled the fish to shore and shared breakfast together. This must have been a little awkward. Jesus had been crucified and buried, and there they were having breakfast with Him. None of the disciples dared to ask Him about anything. They waited until He initiated a conversation with them.

When they finished their breakfast, Jesus started to speak with Peter. He proceeded to ask Peter, "Do you love Me?" Jesus asked Peter this question three times!

For years, I thought I understood what was going on here. Jesus was giving Peter a chance to make up for the three times Peter denied Him. This was about addressing each time Peter had denied the Lord. But as I got into this story a bit more, I realized it wasn't that. Let's read how the conversation went:

> So when they had eaten breakfast, Jesus said to Simon Peter, "Simon, son of Jonah, do you love Me more than these?"
> He said to Him, "Yes, Lord; You know that I love You."
> He said to him, "Feed My lambs."
> He said to him again a second time, "Simon, son of Jonah, do you love Me?"
> He said to Him, "Yes, Lord; You know that I love You."
> He said to him, "Tend My sheep."
> He said to him the third time, "Simon, son of Jonah, do you love Me?" Peter was grieved because He said to him the third time, "Do you love Me?"
> And he said to Him, "Lord, You know all things; You know that I love You."
> Jesus said to him, "Feed My sheep. Most assuredly, I say to you, when you were younger, you girded yourself and walked where you wished; but when you are old, you will stretch out your hands, and another will gird you and carry you where you do not wish." (Jn. 21:15–18)

What I believe Jesus was doing here was breaking the shame off Peter and bringing him back into relationship by letting Peter realize who he really was: a lover of Jesus.

Jesus looked Peter in the eyes and said, "Do you love Me?"

Peter knew that deep down he loved Jesus and answered, "Yes, Lord, I love You."

And I imagine Jesus smiled and said, "Yes, Peter, I know you love Me. That is who you are. You are not defined by your failures. You are more than that. Say it again. Tell Me, do you love Me?"

"Yes, Lord, I love You."

Jesus then affirmed, "You do! That is who you are. Say it one more time."

Jesus was bringing Peter back. This was not about getting even, not about paying for his sins. This was about identity and restoration. And something grew inside Peter. It was the assurance that he was not defined by his sins, that there was something more to him than his shortcomings. He was a lover of Jesus! Perhaps his love was weak or immature, but it was still love. And it was real.

After these questions, Jesus started talking to Peter about Peter's future ministry.

Jesus had taught Peter some very important lessons. Peter had to learn that his strength didn't rest in his commitment to Jesus but in Jesus' commitment to him.

Peter was not to put confidence in his ability to follow Jesus but in Jesus' ability to lead him. Peter was not going to make it because he was such an awesome follower of Jesus but because Jesus was such an awesome leader of weak and broken disciples.

Jesus had never given up on Peter. He knew exactly how immature and weak Peter was, and He prayed for Peter. Jesus loved Peter through all his mistakes. Jesus was not waiting for him to grow up; no, Jesus was committed to Peter through the process.

Legalism teaches us that it's our commitment to God that motivates Him to be committed to us. Grace teaches us that it's God's commitment to us that enables us to be committed to Him.

So, we leave Peter now in a much better place.

Peter	Shulamite	You
☺	☹	☹

Now, let's go back to the Song of Songs where we find our Shulamite.

The Shulamite

The Shulamite was overly conscious of her shortcomings. Ashamed, she lost sight of the king. When we left her, she had just asked how to find the king again. All she wanted was to go back to the time when she first felt captivated by love, but she couldn't break out of the negative emotion. She couldn't overlook her darkness. And just like Peter, she needed someone to reach out to her and pull her out of her shame.

In Song of Songs 1:8, Solomon spoke for the first time in the book, and he spoke right into her situation:

> If you do not know, O fairest among women,
> Follow in the footsteps of the flock,
> And feed your little goats
> Beside the shepherds' tents.

The king stepped in and declared over her how he saw her. To him, the Shulamite was the most beautiful of women. He loved her as she was. He spoke truth over her heart and then proceeded to give her instructions on how to find him. As Jesus brought Peter back to the liberty of a loving relationship, King Solomon brought the Shulamite back into the same freedom.

Peter	Shulamite	You
☺	☺	☹

You

What about you? Unless you live in complete denial, you understand to some degree what Peter and the Shulamite went through. You are aware of your shortcomings. And your heart yearns to experience that same grace.

As Jesus was committed to Peter, He is committed to you. God is not sitting back on His throne waiting for you to get your stuff sorted out. He has no problem stepping into the messiness of your life and leading you into the freedom of His love. He loves you in the journey. He is praying for you (Heb. 7:25). Yes, you may be weak and immature, but that is not the main point. He loves you, and as weak as you may feel, you are a lover of God.

Don't run off in your shame. God wants to lift your chin and look you in the eyes and say a few things to you.

Jesus is found in every book of the Bible. On the road to Emmaus, Jesus taught two disciples about Himself from every book in the Old Testament (Lk. 24:27). In Song of Songs, King Solomon is a picture of Jesus. This book sheds light on the emotions of God toward His people. Song of Songs 4:9 is one example. As you read it, imagine God speaking these words to you:

> You have ravished my heart,
> My sister, my spouse;
> You have ravished my heart
> With one look of your eyes.

God is deeply emotional. When you got saved, you didn't become just another name in the records of heaven. No, God felt something about it. He loved you then, and He loves you now. You don't have to pray and fast for days to get noticed in heaven. One glance of your eyes heavenward God will treasure for eternity.

The bride in Song of Songs declares: "I am my beloved's, and his desire is toward me" (7:10).

Jesus loves you. And His desire is toward you. Right now.

You, the Shulamite, and Peter are happy once again as you realize you are loved in your messiest messes and weakest weaknesses.

Peter   Shulamite   You
☺   ☺   ☺

Going Deeper

1. Do you see yourself as someone who loves God?
2. Do you think a good completion of your life will depend mostly on your ability to do good or on God's grace?
3. Do you really believe God can love and enjoy you despite your weaknesses and shortcomings? That He loves and accepts you as you are?
4. How do you think God responds to sincere Christians who are disappointed and ashamed by their brokenness?
5. If your own child were burdened by shame for not acting like an adult, what would you tell him or her?

Meditation Verses:

Song of Songs 1:8; 4:9; 7:10

9

Loved in Weakness

In Luke 7:19–23, an interesting situation is described. It's a story involving John the Baptist. Time had passed since John had baptized Jesus. John was now in prison, and his ministry was coming to an end while Jesus' ministry was taking off. It was at this place that John learned what the Shulamite learned years before and what Peter and you learned much later—namely, how consistently Jesus loves us even when we are not doing so well.

Calling two of his disciples to himself, John sent them to Jesus to ask Jesus whether He was the promised Messiah or if they should look for someone else. Now, that was a little strange when you think about it, right? I mean, if there was one person on the earth who had to be certain about the identity of Jesus Christ, I would think that would be John. His whole life's mission was to announce the coming of Jesus, to prepare the way for Him. At an earlier time, John had told the crowds about Jesus' coming and had publicly identified Jesus. And John had baptized Jesus. John had stood right there in the water with Jesus after His baptism when the heavens above opened, and John had seen the dove descending on Jesus. Then, John had heard the Father speak from heaven, saying: "'You are My beloved Son; in You I am well pleased'" (Lk. 3:22).

John's being in prison must have been rough. No one likes prison. John was a bit of a wild man, used to his life in the wilderness, eating animals and sleeping under the stars. Then he ended up in a prison cell. Surely, that was not a part of his future life goals. But there he was, nonetheless. His life was not working out as expected.

In Luke 7, it appears John was wondering what was going on, trying to make sense of his hard circumstances. He was questioning everything, doubting whether this whole thing with Jesus was real.

The two disciples John sent went to Jesus, and I can just picture it. Maybe they were a little embarrassed. "Uh, Jesus, John the Baptist has sent us to You to ask, 'Are You are the Coming One, or should we look for another?' It's John's question."

And you would think Jesus would have gone off on John. After all, God doesn't like it when we ask Him if He's for real, right? This is How to Get Rebuked by God 101, isn't it?

Jesus didn't rebuke John, though. Jesus didn't pull His hair out or pluck His beard in total desperation. He didn't even drop His shoulders in disappointment.

Instead, Jesus was very kind and encouraged John. At that moment, Jesus was busy healing the sick and casting out demons, and He said to John's disciples: "'Go and tell John the things you have seen and heard: that the blind see, the lame walk, the lepers are cleansed, the deaf hear, the dead are raised, the poor have the gospel preached to them'" (Lk. 7:22). When Jesus said this, He was quoting from messianic prophecies in Isaiah, passages with which John was familiar (see Isa. 35:5; 61:1–3). Jesus was saying, "Look, I am fulfilling the prophecies before your eyes. I am the One."

Jesus then ended His message to John with these words, "'And blessed is he who is not offended because of Me'" (Lk. 7:23).

Offended! It is amazing how easily we get offended with God

when life does not go as we thought it should. When things get hard, we tend to blame God.

I remember sitting next to Marlies as she was in labor with our first child. It was unbelievable. I was sitting there seeing her struggle through twenty-four hours of agony, and I got so mad at God. I couldn't believe He was letting my wife suffer like that. Of course, I forgot all about it once we had our child.

Hitting the Wall

I hit the wall during my time as a missionary in Kenya. We had felt led by God to organize a large prayer gathering in the Nyayo National Stadium in Nairobi, the capital city. It was a big step of faith for our little organization. The finances alone were crazy. The cost of that single day was enough to run our whole ministry for three years! However, we were excited. God had spoken to our hearts to hold the gathering, and our hearts were full of faith.

Right after we had chosen to hold this day of prayer and fasting, election time came around. The two presidential candidates represented the two largest tribes in the country. The controversial outcome lit a spark to the underlying tribal tension in the country, and violence broke out across the nation. The two tribes of the presidential candidates started fighting each other, and other tribes chose sides.

Roadblocks were set up on major roads, and groups of people would check vehicles for people from the opposing tribe. Many would be pulled out of their cars and hacked to death with machetes right there. Hundreds of thousands of people were displaced as they fled the violence. Around eight hundred churches were burned to the ground by their own church members simply because the pastor was from an opposing tribe. The country was in chaos. Airports closed down, and people all over the world were watching on TV how this otherwise peaceful and stable nation was self-destructing. The division along tribal lines became painfully visible.

Marlies and I lived in Kitale at this time, and we were breeding a few watchdogs. A man who lived an hour away from us had recently purchased one of our adult dogs, and at night he would let him roam around in his fenced yard to guard his house. One morning during this time of post-election violence, he woke up and went outside to be greeted by his dog. He then walked over to his gate, which had an opening in it so that you could pull the latch to open the door from the outside. When he got there, he saw blood on his gate, and to his disgust, he saw two fingers lying there in his yard. He opened his gate and saw several clubs and machetes lying on the ground.

At night, gangs of people would go around from house to house, looking for people from the opposing tribe and seeking to rape the wife and kill the husband. This man was from a minority tribe in his city, and they probably had come to attack him that night. Most likely, as one of the attackers had tried to open the gate from the outside, the dog had bitten off two of his fingers, causing the intruder and those with him to flee.

This man loved our dog!

Finally, the government was able to restore peace and bring an end to the violence. As everyone was reeling from this nationwide outburst of brutality, Marlies and I realized that this day of prayer and fasting seemed more needed than ever. So, we moved from our small town in Western Kenya to the capital city and started mobilizing and preparing for the big day of prayer.

The time was right. When we decided to call for this day of prayer and fasting, of course, we never expected the aftermath of the elections to expose the division in the country and result in such horrific violence. In early 2008, Kenya had given the world a glimpse into its troubling lack of unity. At the end of 2008, we realized our scheduled day of prayer would provide us with an opportunity to show the world that, from all of this, the church could come together across denominational and tribal lines, and stand united before God.

The vice president of the country decided to attend our event and publicly repented. He committed the country to God. (I'm not sure to what degree that counts since he wasn't the president, but we embraced his message and joined in committing the nation to God.) Key leaders from different denominations wept together. Parents reconciled with their children. Young and old cried out together for God to have mercy on their nation. And it became a powerful day of united prayer. It was broadcast live on TV in Kenya and on Christian TV all over the world. The unity around this event was incredible.

As the day was progressing, I started to feel discouraged, and I couldn't shake it. Of course, I kept going, but by the time the day was over, I felt a heaviness on me. I felt like a total failure. I went to bed deeply discouraged.

That started a challenging season when I felt like everything had fallen apart. I became depressed and would lie on my bed, curtains closed, phone switched off, watching movies and eating. Friends would try to encourage me about the prayer day being a success, but it just didn't get through to me.

I know this might not make any sense to you. It didn't make any sense to those around me at the time. Even my friends and family found it difficult to understand what was going on inside me, especially since many things with the event had gone so well. But depression doesn't always make sense.

We had one child at the time—our three-year-old son. The day after the gathering, he started to stutter horribly. He had never had a problem talking, but he woke up the day after the event and was barely able to form words.

I was not a fun person to be around in the weeks that followed. Tensions grew between my wife and me.

I was convinced my ministry was over. I felt like a failed missionary. My marriage didn't feel good. My child couldn't talk anymore. Marlies and I had no money left. We couldn't even drive our car because we couldn't afford the insurance on it.

At that point, I decided it was time for my "plan B." For many years, I always had a plan B. In case God fired me or I messed up as a missionary, I was determined I could become a scuba diving instructor. I loved diving, and when life didn't work out, I figured I simply would hide under water. So, I started looking online for jobs on the coast of Kenya where there was great diving.

Help Arrives

One month into my depression, a few people from Canada came to see me. I have to tell you about them. Their names are John and Eloise Bergen. They are a Canadian couple in their late sixties who at an earlier time had moved to our town of Kitale to be missionaries and dedicate the remainder of their lives to ministering to children at risk. They are an amazing, godly couple, humble and compassionate. Only a year earlier, before our prayer gathering, on an evening at around nine o'clock at night, John had been walking around in his yard. He was enjoying the cool weather and all the sounds of an African village. Suddenly, a gang of seven people broke into his property and assaulted him.

Using big machetes, the gang started hacking into him and beating him up. They broke bones and made huge cuts all over his body. Finally, they picked up his body and threw it into the bushes, leaving him for dead. But they weren't finished with their rampage. They proceeded into John's house only to find Eloise bathing. They raped her and tied her up, also beating her with their machetes. Thank God, miraculously, both John and Eloise survived!

By an airplane ambulance, the Bergens were transported to a hospital in the capital city of Nairobi to be taken care of. After the attack, I remember going to their house to gather a few belongings for them to take on the plane. I saw the blood on the floor. The whole missionary community in our town was in shock, to put it mildly. While the Bergens fought for their lives in the hospital in Nairobi, the national media of Canada reported the brutal attack on the missionaries.

After spending several weeks in the hospital in Nairobi, they were strong enough to be transported to Canada for further recovery. As their bodies were healing, God was also working on their hearts and brought incredible emotional healing. He took them on a journey of forgiveness, too.

Meanwhile, the authorities in Kenya believed they had caught the criminals and asked the Bergens to come back to testify against their attackers in court. They decided to come back. John said he wanted to take the opportunity to look his attackers in the eyes and tell them he had forgiven them and God loved them.

And so, one year after the horrific attack, John and Eloise boarded a plane and flew back to Kenya. I was one month into my depression when they arrived. Upon landing in Nairobi, they heard I wasn't doing well and decided to come and see Marlies and me. I vividly remember sitting in a small room with them around a table. John sat to the right of me, and Eloise sat across from me at the table. And they proceeded to ask how we were doing.

The fact was, I was disappointed. I had expected more from the prayer gathering—more participants and a greater manifestation of God's power. Later, I understood my original disappointment was compounded by an attack from the enemy, by lies he interjected into the situation. I believed the entire prayer gathering was a failure, and God had let it all happen. I offloaded on John and Eloise, telling them how God told me to do the prayer rally and then how He had let me fail. I said it didn't make sense to me and explained I was feeling very discouraged. John graciously listened to me emote and then gently asked, "Can I pray for you?"

"Sure," I mumbled, thinking, *Whatever. Do what you want to do.* And that was how I felt. I had no hope.

John laid his hand on me and quietly started to cry. And he said, "Daniel, I am so sorry for what you are going through."

I opened my eyes for a little while and looked at Eloise across from me. She partially smiled at me—her face and jaw were still disfigured from the attack. Looking into her eyes, I realized they had experienced one of the worst things I could imagine, and whatever was happening with me started to seem small in comparison. That opened my heart to receive, and as John prayed for me, something happened. I can't really explain it, but God touched me and did something real.

John finished praying, and I stood up. I felt different. I felt physically lighter. I felt like I had lost a good amount of weight. The heaviness had lifted. That day marked the beginning of a journey where God would bring healing to areas in my life that needed it. Little by little, day by day, God pulled me out of depression and discouragement.

At the same time, I had a hard time trusting God since I felt that He had let me fall and had abandoned me. For months, I didn't go to church. I just couldn't do it.

Soon, we moved back to our home in Kitale. (We had only moved to Nairobi for six months to organize the prayer gathering.) For two months, day after day, I would wake up, walk over to my office, and sit there. I felt completely empty. I had nothing to offer God. There was no song, no prayer, no nothing. And I would tell God, "I'm just here, and I don't know what to do."

We had been missionaries in Kenya for five years up until that time, and I had never really taken a break. I had been running until I couldn't anymore. We had been praying and seeking God for revival in Kenya. I had read about the great East African Revival, and we longed to see God again powerfully visit this nation we loved so much. But things were looking very different. I had never imagined I would find myself in such a depression.

Looking once again at Luke 7, after Jesus had answered John's question, the two disciples went back to the prison where John was kept, and they reported to him what Jesus had said.

In the meantime, Jesus turned to the crowd that surrounded Him and started to speak to them about John the Baptist. I expected

Jesus to take that opportunity to teach the people a lesson from John's lack of faith and clarity. I surmised Jesus could have encouraged the people to not be like John but always to believe in Him.

But Jesus didn't do that. Instead, He honored John publicly. He told everyone how great He thought John was. Jesus said that, up to that moment in history, no man born to a woman was greater than John! That's not a bad endorsement coming from God Himself!

And I love this. Jesus honored John in his weakest moment. God is like that. He loves us at our weakest or most vulnerable moments.

Going Deeper

1. Search your heart—is there any offense in your heart toward God over things that have happened in your life?
2. Do you feel like you can fully trust God, or are there reservations in your heart? Why do you think you have a hard time trusting Him related to that area of your life?
3. Was there a moment in your life when you felt down, and God used someone to minister to you?
4. Jesus was so gracious with John the Baptist. Looking back, what have been moments that God was gracious to you?

Meditation Verses:

Luke 7:19–28
Psalm 145:8–9

10

A Different Perspective

God is not intimidated by our pain or our sinfulness. He has no problem stepping into the messiness of our lives to bring healing and freedom. As we've learned together, when we have a wrong picture of God, we tend to run away from Him instead of to Him, especially when we sin or things get ugly. We deny God access, and our hearts shut down.

A few months after I got depressed, Marlies and I decided we needed a break. In the time that followed, God stepped into my messiness and brought healing and understanding.

Trusting God

The first thing I had to do was choose to trust God and not be offended—especially when life didn't make sense. I had to believe God was still good. Nahum 1:7 says that the Lord is good. It makes sense that if He *is* good, and He is always Himself, then He is *always* good.

Sometimes, to experience the peace that surpasses our understanding, we have to give up the right to understand. Scripture tells us, "'For as the heavens are higher than the earth, so are My ways higher than your ways, and My thoughts than your thoughts'" (Isa. 55:9). God's ways are higher than our ways, His thoughts higher than ours. Things are probably going to happen in your life that you won't fully understand. And that is okay because, if God and His ways were small enough for you to fully understand, then He wouldn't be big enough to trust with your life. Let God be God. And let Him be greater than you can comprehend.

Of course, it is not wrong to seek understanding, but I found that, typically, faith comes before understanding. Understanding, then, comes to a heart that trusts God.

Also, I had to learn to look to God for encouragement and approval. God doesn't measure our success by numbers but by obedience. He asks us to obey Him. Obviously, He wants us to bear fruit, but we usually don't do a great job measuring it.

Our primary focus is to love and obey God. We live for Him, and He sees what we do. God loves our sincere efforts even when they are small in the world's eyes. Don't compare yourself to others, and don't despise small beginnings. God sees your work, and He rejoices in it.

Zechariah wrote, "'For who has despised the day of small things? For these seven rejoice to see the plumb line in the hand of Zerubbabel. They are the eyes of the LORD, which scan to and fro throughout the whole earth'" (4:10). Instead of seeking encouragement in the amount of good works that we are doing and the things we are accomplishing, we must seek true encouragement the only place it is found—in experiencing God's pleasure over our sincere efforts.

Faithfulness

As a missionary in Kenya, I often struggled with discouragement. Marlies and I frequently had people visiting us to see how and what we were doing. So, I would take them around and show them

A DIFFERENT PERSPECTIVE

what we had been working on. For the most part, what we were doing felt small and insignificant. I came to Africa to see God move in power! I wanted to see another East African Revival! I came for the "big things" that thus far weren't so big. It was a little embarrassing. I would always catch myself making excuses for why everything was still so small. Most of the time, people would respond by saying, "No, Daniel, what you are doing is great! You've done so much in such a short time. There are a lot of good things going on here."

Yes, God was moving. The Lord really was doing things, but in my estimation our work felt small. People continued to encourage me by pointing out the fruit of our work, but their kindness in doing so never affected my perspective.

Now, looking back, I wish someone would have visited us and actually agreed with me that it was small then, but also told me not to despise small beginnings. I needed someone to direct my heart into the pleasure of God and away from my sincere little efforts.

Of course, we can celebrate the fruit of our works. True encouragement, however, comes not from looking at the works of our hands but from connecting with God's heart. He smiles over our lives. We live for God. We live for His approval. Our goal is to be obedient. At the end of the day, all that matters is God saying, "Well done, good and faithful servant" (Mt. 25:21, 23; Lk. 19:17). So, we want to posture our hearts in faithful obedience to God.

Faithfulness is not a popular word. It sounds so boring. But it is a big deal to God. When you read through the New Testament, you will find that believers were often called *faithful*.

- Timothy ... faithful son in the Lord. (1 Cor. 4:17)
- To the saints who are in Ephesus, and faithful in Christ Jesus ... (Eph. 1:1)
- To the saints and faithful brethren in Christ who are in Colosse ... (Col. 1:2)
- Epaphras, our dear fellow servant, who is a faithful minister of Christ ... (Col. 1:7)

- Tychicus, a beloved brother, faithful minister, and fellow servant in the Lord ... (Col. 4:7)
- Onesimus, a faithful and beloved brother ... (Col. 4:9)
- Silvanus, our faithful brother ... (1 Pet. 5:12)

Not only were believers often called *faithful*, God Himself is: "He who calls you is faithful, who also will do it" (1 Thes. 5:24).

God greatly values faithfulness. And if He does, we would do well to value it also.

In Matthew 25, Jesus told the famous parable about the man who, before leaving on a journey, gave his servants talents. When the man came back, he honored those who had taken the little given them and faithfully gone to work with it. The man said, "Well done, good and faithful servant; you were faithful over a few things, I will make you ruler over many things" (Mt. 25:21, 23).

Instead of waiting to be made a ruler over many things, we would do best to be faithful with the little things. In fact, being faithful with the little things is like a test that reveals your heart, because Jesus knows that he who is faithful with what is least is also faithful with much.

It's embarrassing to admit it, but I don't like being faithful with what is least. It just doesn't look good. I don't know about you, but I'd rather be faithful with the "big and spectacular." But God is testing us. What will we do with the small things? Will we remain faithful? When we feel like quitting but choose to keep going because we know it's right, we grow in faithfulness.

One of my favorite quotes comes from Hudson Taylor. He said, "A little thing is a little thing, but faithfulness in little things is a great thing."[1] This reminds us that we don't have to be involved in the "big stuff" to be great in the eyes of God. Faithfully continue with what God has entrusted to you in this season of your life. And don't "grow weary while doing good, for in due season [you] shall reap if [you] do not lose heart" (Gal. 6:9).

Many Christians, especially charismatic Christians, are hoping and waiting and praying for a breakthrough moment, a special encounter where they receive much grace and it takes them at once to where they desire to be. But their expectation often exists in the absence of a commitment to faithfulness in the little, and they fail to recognize the importance and fruit of building faithfully day by day. Waiting for breakthrough has kept many Christians from living a disciplined life of prayer and study of the Word. They have not given themselves to daily living and growing in faithfulness but are only focusing on the desired breakthrough.

Please don't dismiss the importance of engaging faithfully and prayerfully in what God has currently entrusted you with. Breakthrough is best received by a faithful heart, because faithful hearts best steward the gifts of God.

Thankfulness

One of the other things God was teaching me during those years in Kenya was to cultivate a thankful heart. If you are an entitled Christian who is offended with God and feels like God owes you, you have really lost perspective. God owes us nothing. And all He has done has been grace. He has given us more than we could have ever earned. Sometimes, we lose sight of that.

I want to live with a grateful heart, living in the wonder of God's grace and goodness to me. But that does not come naturally to me. For some reason, I tend to focus on what I don't have and what I think I need.

It is difficult for seeds of discouragement to take root in the soil of a thankful heart. And there is always reason for thanksgiving. You may not always be able to discern what the Lord is doing now, but you can always recall what He has done in the past. When you feel discouraged or upset with your circumstances, it's time to recall the good things the Lord has done in your life. Encourage yourself in your history with the Lord and His commitment to you.

The apostle Paul told the Philippians he was "confident of this very thing, that He who has begun a good work in you will complete it until the day of Jesus Christ" (Phil. 1:6). We also should be confident of this. Consider the good things God has done in your life, and assure yourself that He is going to keep being good to you. He will bring His work in your life to completion. God will never quit on you. He is not walking away from you.

If you have a hard time thinking of something good the Lord has done for you, let me give you something to consider afresh: Jesus died an agonizing death for you. He found you worth dying for. He loved you to the point of death. Hanging on that cross, He put the love of your heavenly Father on display for all the world to see. And when He hung on that cross, you were the joy set before Him to endure the suffering (Heb. 12:2). You were His happy thought. He did this while we were still enemies of God. As Charles Spurgeon said, "Sit before the cross and watch the dying Savior till faith springs up spontaneously in your heart. There is no place like Calvary for creating confidence. The air of that sacred hill brings health to trembling faith."[2] Discouragement is a loss of perspective, and it is in the face of Jesus Christ that we gain perspective.

God is good and always better than you think He is. And He is always doing more than you can see. We don't see most of the good God does, although sometimes it's as if He lifts a veil and shows us a little bit of what happens behind the scenes. That happened one time with my wife and me.

Behind the Scenes

When Marlies was three months pregnant with our second child, she started bleeding and feeling contractions. We were still living in Kenya then, and I called a doctor to ask what this meant. The doctor told me over the phone that this was the beginning of a miscarriage. He said our child had died, and my wife would give birth to the dead fetus. I was shocked and asked what we had to do. He told us we could stay home and then explained what we could expect to happen. Lastly, he told me to call him again if I needed to.

I told my wife the bad news, and later that day we lost our child. We didn't know what gender our child was, so we had not selected a name. We still wanted to name this child of ours, though. We prayed, and my wife said, "Justice—that name just came to mind." So we named our child Justice and thanked the Lord for our gift, as short as life had been for him or her.

While Marlies was still upstairs in our bedroom, having continued contractions, I went downstairs to get some water from the kitchen. All of a sudden, I heard her scream my name, *"Daniel!"*

I ran upstairs and found Marlies lying unconscious in the bathroom. She had fainted and had felt it coming on, so she had called me right before she went unconscious. I sat next to her as she regained consciousness. But after a while, she fainted again and kept on going in and out of consciousness. Meanwhile, she was losing a lot of blood, and it got real messy. I was thinking what she was experiencing wasn't normal. So, I called the doctor again and explained what was happening.

The doctor said that this was not normal and not good. He said we needed to get my wife to the hospital "ASAP." But the good hospital was about an hour-and-a-half's drive from our house on a bad, bumpy road, and my wife was in no condition then to travel. There was a little primitive clinic five minutes from our house, and I decided to take her there.

When we arrived, I told the doctor what was happening, and the staff immediately took Marlies to the operating theater. The doctor said they would put her to sleep and might have to operate on her. I was so nervous. I had no idea what they were going to do. And this place looked more like a place where you would contract a disease rather than get healed of one. My only thought was to tell the doctor to use clean needles. When I did, he laughed and assured me they would.

I stood next to Marlies as she was stretched out on the table. The doctor and nurses were getting things ready, and when the anesthetist was about to sedate her, I heard her pray, "Lord, please let the doctor be a Christian." Right at that moment the doctor's phone rang, and the ringtone was that of the worship song, "As the Deer." Marlies smiled, and the anesthetist placed the mask on her face to put her to sleep. The doctor told me to leave the room and wait outside.

Outside, I immediately called my friend Matthew in the Netherlands. I told him we just lost our child, and Marlies was not well and in the operating theater. I explained that we didn't know what was wrong and didn't even know what the medical team was going to do with her. He quickly gathered some friends, and they started to pray for us.

About twenty-five minutes later, Marlies was wheeled to a room with one bed where they laid her, and I could stay with her. The doctor told me what had happened and what they had done and said not to worry. She would be able to have children in the future and would fully recover. He said she'd wake up in about thirty minutes. The nurses tucked her in, and there was my wife, lying on her back, eyes closed, completely knocked out from the anesthetics. The nurses left, and I sat on the one chair in the room staring at Marlies.

Within minutes, I heard her whisper, "Dan, Dan . . ."

I thought, *She is waking up already?* So, I got right up close to her and asked, "Marlies, are you okay?"

But she didn't respond and kept her eyes closed. A little later, again, she said, "Dan, Dan . . ."

"Yes, I'm here, Marlies." Same thing. She didn't respond to anything I said.

Out of nowhere, with a strong voice, her eyes still closed and still lying on her back, she said, "I see him. I see our little child. It's a boy." Then, she proceeded to describe him, and she continued to describe what she was seeing, "I see the Father take our little child, and He's holding him."

There was a short pause, and then she said, "Jesus, Jesus, You are so beautiful." Marlies began to weep, and over and over she said, "Jesus, You're so beautiful. Jesus, You're so beautiful." Her face was shining as she was lying there with tears running down her cheeks.

At this point, I realized something was happening. She didn't respond to me. She kept her eyes closed, and I was wondering if she was in heaven. If she were seeing Jesus, then maybe she was almost dead or something. That thought made me very nervous. As a result, I went to look for the doctor and told him that Marlies was talking but not responding. I asked him to come and check on her. The doctor told me to calm down, looked at his watch, and said it would be another twenty minutes or so until she would wake up.

Still a bit shaken, I went back to the room. Then, a nurse came in. I wondered if the doctor had sent her to make sure Marlies was all right. The nurse addressed Marlies in Swahili, and I kindly told the nurse we didn't speak Swahili, asking her if she would speak in English instead. Marlies and I had had some language lessons but were not speaking Swahili as yet. We could say greetings and some little phrases, but that was all we knew. As soon as I finished, Marlies turned her head toward the nurse and, with her eyes still closed, started speaking to the nurse in fluent Swahili. I couldn't fully understand her, but I recognized she was saying some of the names of God and was saying something about Him. I must have come across as a little dumb. I had no sooner told the nurse Marlies didn't speak Swahili when Marlies was suddenly speaking the language—and speaking it fluently! The nurse left, and I never saw her again.

For twenty minutes more, Marlies continued to describe all she saw. She even began to prophesy over me, people on our team, and Kenya. And every time in between her prophetic utterances, she kept saying how beautiful Jesus was. Then, she got quiet for about five minutes, at which time she opened her eyes and woke up. I asked her if she was okay, and she said she was thirsty. I got her some water.

Marlies remembered nothing of all she spoke except having a

mental image of our child. It was incredible!

Soon, my friend from the Netherlands, Matthew, called me. He said, "Daniel, you have to talk to my wife." The next thing I heard was the choked up voice of Matthew's wife in my ear. Crying, she told me they had been praying and that she had seen a vision, "I think I saw your child. I think it was a boy. And I think his name was Justice."

"I think you're right," I responded. "That was our child." I was stunned. I had not told them about the name or anything.

The next day, we left the clinic. It was so sad that we had lost our child. Yet, at the same time, God had been so powerfully present in the midst of us and brought us such comfort through Marlies's experience and the phone call from Matthew in the Netherlands. Marlies and I realized that, when she miscarried, it was as if she gave birth directly into the arms of God. Our son is the first one of our family who made it to heaven. He lives in the direct presence of God.

There is an old hymn called "It Is Well with My Soul." You may have heard of it or even sung it. The story behind the song is powerful.[3] It was written by a man called Horatio Spafford. He was a successful and wealthy lawyer living in Chicago in the 1800s. He was married to his wife, Anna, and together they had five kids, one son and four daughters. Horatio was a friend of the famous evangelist Dwight L. Moody.

In 1871, at the height of his career, Horatio and Anna suffered the loss of their only son. The same year of their son's death, the Great Chicago Fire burned up almost all of his real estate investments. This was a huge blow to what he had been building for many years.

Horatio and his wife decided they needed a break and chose to go to England. Dwight L. Moody was holding crusades there, and they thought they would join him. So, they booked passage aboard a ship to make the crossing across the Atlantic Ocean, but then a last-minute business crisis made Horatio stay behind to take care of his business before following his wife and daughters to England.

Four days into the journey, the ship had a collision with another ship, and it started to take on water.

Anna took her four daughters to the deck and together they prayed as the ship started sinking. All four daughters drowned. Anna was able to hold on to some wreckage and was later found by a fisherman. She survived. She sent word to her husband, and Horatio boarded the first boat out to meet his broken wife.

Four days into the journey, the captain called for Horatio to come to his cabin, and he told Horatio that they were over the waters where the ship had sunk and all four of his daughters had drowned.

Horatio went to his room, and that was when he wrote those now famous words to this hymn.

> When peace, like a river, attendeth my way,
> When sorrows like sea billows roll;
> Whatever my lot, Thou has taught me to say,
> "It is well, it is well with my soul."[4]

That is great faith. That is a confidence in God so deep, even life's greatest hurts don't wash it away.[5]

Going Deeper

1. What has been an experience in your life that doesn't make sense but where you can choose to trust God anyways?
2. What are some things you know God has called you to that you really want to be faithful in?
3. Take some time to thank God.

Meditation Verses:

Isaiah 55:9
Philippians 1:6
Psalm 107:1

Part 3

Learning to Love

11

Love, the Way of Holiness

Two American friends of mine just married. They made a wonderful couple and had a beautiful wedding. Even though I officiated the wedding, it was still an American wedding and different than what I was used to having grown up in the Netherlands. Dutch weddings are typically longer, though the procession at the start is shorter.

Whenever I attend weddings, I can't help but remember my wedding day. Though it has been a while, I still remember that day vividly. I was very nervous—the most nervous I had ever been in my life. At the same time, I was very excited. I had worked hard to earn all the money needed and looked forward to marrying. Finally, the day came, and Marlies was going to be my wife. I'd have her! It was my day of victory!

Of course, I had to wear a suit. I am not much of a suit kind of guy, but I couldn't get out of wearing one for our wedding. Suit, tie, polished shoes—everything was in place when the service was about to start. I was seated in the front by the aisle, and next to me sat my best man. The rest of the room was filled with all our friends and family.

Soon, the music began to play. I was the first to stand up, my best man stood up right after me, and then everyone in the room stood up. We were all looking to the back of the room. My heart was racing as the doors slowly opened. Two little flower girls walked through the door and down the aisle. I was not interested in them and kept focusing on that door. And, then, Marlies appeared, holding arms with her father. As she stepped forward into the aisle, she looked perfect. She was beautiful—her hair was just beautiful, her dress was amazing, and she didn't wear too much makeup. As Marlies walked down the aisle, I was staring at her, and she was looking at me until she and her dad reached me at the front of the church. Her dad "delivered the package" to me, may have mumbled a few threats, and the service began. We got married that day, and it was a great day.

But I've been thinking, *What if something different would have happened?*

An Unfaithful Bride Imagined

Imagine with me, if you will, the wedding music begins to play, everybody stands and looks at the back doors opening as two little flower girls who nobody is interested in walk down the aisle. Next, Marlies appears, and she looks great, and she and her father start walking down the aisle toward me. The church is full of young people. (We got married pretty young and were some of the first among our group of friends to get married.) There are lots of young single guys in the room, and I am sure some of them are wishing they were getting married today. However, it is *my* day of victory!

Imagine again Marlies walking down the aisle, and about halfway down, while on her way to me, she looks to the right, sees this really handsome young man, and says, "Dad, wait a minute." She pulls out a pen and paper from her wedding dress pocket (just humor me here), writes down her phone number, and says to this guy she thought was handsome, "Hey, this is my number. Maybe give me a call later tonight. I'd love to get together. I'm a little busy today, but I'd love to get to know you a little more," as she winks. (That would be crazy, right?!) I stand there, thinking, *What is going on?* I try to make sense of it all, but before I can wrap my mind around it, she comes back to the aisle, to her dad, and she continues walking toward me. And, then, she looks to the left! She notices this other guy and walks toward him. Before I know it, she is sitting on his lap and kissing him!

Obviously, if that would have happened, we would have had to cancel the wedding. That would have not been my day!

Now, I know this sounds ridiculous, but I want to compare this to our relationship with the Lord Jesus. We as the Church, as God's people, are the Bride of Christ. On the day Marlies was my bride, as she walked down that aisle, her heart didn't go out to any other guys. There were plenty of great guys there, but she looked at me, and she married me!

Hebrews 12:1–2 says that we are to run this race of life with our eyes fixed on Jesus. Just as Marlies walked down the aisle looking at me, we want to walk through life with our eyes focused on Jesus. Just as Marlies walked to the front of the church and appeared before me, and our wedding ceremony began, one day at the end of your life, you will appear face to face before Jesus. And you will spend the rest of eternity with Him.

In our lives, many things compete for the attention of our hearts. Both things *and* people try hard to capture the gaze of the eyes of our hearts. When I appear before God, whenever that day comes, I want to be able to say, "Lord, here is my heart. I have kept it for You. You are number one. I love You more than anyone or anything else."

Christianity is not a sin management program but a relationship. It is not a system of rules; it is loving a person. Holiness is loving God with an undivided heart. As M. P. Horban said, "True holiness is learning to enjoy friendship with God."[1]

When I proposed to my wife, she (thankfully) said *yes* wholeheartedly. She didn't ask for any exceptions. She didn't ask me if she could be my wife for 364 days of the year but have one day off per year to hang out and spend the night with this other man she also liked. If she had asked for that, I would have said *no*. Of course, I don't want to share her with any other man. I am jealous for her.

God is jealous for you. He gave everything for you so that you could do the same in return—live fully abandoned to Him. You were designed to live that way. You were made to live wholeheartedly.

Holy Living

When we live a holy life, we are living the way we were made to live.

If you view holiness as this list of things you have to do but don't really want to, and sin as a list of things you are not allowed to do but would want to do, you are not seeing things rightly. You have to understand that holiness is beautiful, and sin is our enemy. This is why God is against sin in your life. He is not trying to be difficult. It's that He knows the destructive effects of it.

If you were to get on a plane with an instructor who was going to take you parachute jumping for the first time in your life, I am sure that instructor would have you follow a few rules. As the plane reached the right altitude, the instructor would again go over a few of them. He would tell you to put on the backpack with the parachute in it and to secure it tightly. You could be thinking, *I don't like all those instructions and rules. I just want to be free and soar.*

Next thing you know, you throw off that backpack, dash past the instructor, and jump out the open door and off the plane. And you're right. For a moment, you would feel incredibly free. It would be quite a rush! Until you make a powerful landing, that is, on the earth, and all the fun would be over. There are obvious reasons for wearing and securing that parachute. It is the same in the kingdom of God. There is a reason behind every commandment of God.

LOVE, THE WAY OF HOLINESS

Obedience to God is liberating. It really is. And it is rewarding. No one looks back at life and regrets holiness. No one regrets loving God wholeheartedly.

Many people live with the regrets of sin and carry the guilt, shame, and consequences of bad decisions. We know sin can feel good in the moment—otherwise, we wouldn't do it. But it never delivers. It never gives the lasting satisfaction only God gives. Sin doesn't fulfill. And so you will always need more. Sin has this annoying way of taking you further than you wanted to go, and it can get addictive. Sin is sticky, and you can end up stuck and captured by it.

Living within God's boundaries will ensure your heart stays free—free to be yourself and to love God with all you've got! No wonder David said in Psalm 16:6, "The lines have fallen to me in pleasant places."

We were all created with a God-sized hole inside us that only His love can fill. If we don't know Him or His love, we are left empty. Sin, then, is simply what we do when we are not satisfied in God. We all know people eat bad things when they are hungry, and many of us have done so. We have looked for fulfillment and excitement in all the wrong places. John wrote, "If anyone loves the world, the love of the Father is not in him" (1 Jn. 2:15).

The characteristic of people who do not know the love of the Father is that they will love the world. They turn to the world, seeking fulfillment. But the opposite is also true. Those who have experienced the love of the Father won't love the world anymore. They have experienced a superior pleasure.

God is good, and His will is perfect and good and pleasing (Nah. 1:7; Rom. 12:2). The devil will lie to you. Temptation is so tempting because of the false promise it makes that sin can make you happier than God can. Do you believe God's love is better than anything else this world has to offer?

The way of holiness, the way of wholehearted love and devotion to God, is the road to true happiness.

I believe the battle against sin was won two thousand years ago by Jesus on the cross. Our battle is primarily a battle of having faith in God and remaining satisfied in Him.

Now, thankfully, we don't have to try to live a holy life so that one day God may accept us. No, He accepts us now, and understanding this motivates and empowers us to live a holy life. You are a deeply loved child of God. He loves you in the messiness of sanctification. You are on a journey, becoming more and more like Jesus. And God is there every step of the way. He is not waiting for you to arrive at a certain point of maturity, and then He will start loving you. He loves you now. He is not waiting for an improved version of you.

He loves you and enjoys you even with the knowledge of your sins and with the knowledge of your weaknesses. C. S. Lewis said, "[The Christian] does not think God will love us because we are good, but that God will make us good because He loves us."[2]

Don't live under the accusation of the enemy. Your sin is not the deepest thing about you. The devil loves to point out what is wrong with you. He wants you to feel dirty and unworthy, because he knows that when you feel dirty you will act dirty.

There is more grace in God than sin in you. God is not against you; He is for you! If we have a wrong picture of God, then when we struggle with sin, we will run away from Him instead of toward Him.

Your behavior flows out of your belief system. Believe God is worth more than anything else this world has to offer. Believe you are loved, accepted, and enjoyed as you are. And believe you can grow in Christ-likeness.

John the Baptist said Christ must increase, and he, John, must decrease (Jn. 3:30). Don't turn that around, as I so often did. My focus was primarily on me having to decrease, having to die to myself, having to deny the flesh, and having to say no and do better and hope that one day God would increase in my life. Sincere Christians can easily get obsessed with overcoming sin and temptation, and fighting it. And the devil loves when we do this. He would much rather have us focus on what we shouldn't be doing than live fascinated with who God is.

We are called to orient our lives around revelation of who God is: to live our lives with our eyes fixed on Jesus (Heb. 12:1–2); to set our minds on the things that are above (Col. 3:2); to stay focused on His love (Jude 21); to get to know Him more and be thankful for all He has done; and to be confident in the finished work of the cross.

The beautiful reality is that, the more we focus on God and the more He increases in our lives, we will automatically decrease. His Spirit will work in us to produce holiness.

In fact, holiness is a change of heart that is produced by the Holy Spirit. We don't grow in holiness by trying harder. Of course, we put effort into our relationship with God, and there is a place for discipline and making right choices. However, we become more like God by beholding God. You become what you behold. If you focus your mind on God and you seek to fill your life with His presence, the Spirit transforms your heart from the inside out. And then you will experience true freedom. You will experience internal transformation and not merely live under externally imposed restraint.

I am so grateful for what Jesus did on the cross, so grateful for forgiveness. Sin does not wear off. Time does not make guilt go away little by little. But Jesus' blood truly washes us clean. He took our guilt, and there is no condemnation for us. Jesus was condemned, and we were accepted.

Have confidence in what Jesus has done for you!

Receive God's forgiveness. Don't try to earn it.

Forgiveness is a gift you can't earn. And you shouldn't—you don't earn gifts. If I bring Marlies flowers and she runs off to get some money to pay me back, the flowers would no longer be a gift.

Accept what Jesus did. Receive it. It's humbling because there is a part of us that would rather earn it or prefer to do it in our own strength. But humble yourself before God and receive His grace.

God gives grace to the humble, not because the humble earn it, but because the humble are willing to receive it (Jas. 4:6). Hebrews 10:17–18 encourages us in the fact that, once our sins have been forgiven, there is no need to offer any more sacrifices.

So, when you mess up, run to God. Don't be afraid of rejection. God never rejects a broken heart. Brother Lawrence, a seventeenth-century French monk whose inner life with God was described in the classic booklet *The Practice of the Presence of God*, knew something about this:

> Brother Lawrence was aware of his sins and was not at all surprised by them. "That is my nature," he would say, "the only thing I know how to do." He simply confessed his sins to God without pleading with Him or making excuses. After this, he was able to peacefully resume his regular activity of love and adoration. If Brother Lawrence didn't sin, he thanked God for it, because only God's grace could keep him from sinning.³

God's throne is a throne of grace. And grace is what you need. Let your weaknesses and struggles be stepping stones to draw closer to God. They don't disqualify you from His love. We are "wounded and sinful people who are nevertheless caught up in the transforming love of God."⁴

Your confidence before God depends on the cross, not on whether you did well recently. You can draw near despite your brokenness. Near God is where you will find the joy and peace of agreement with Him and the forgiveness of sins.

Going Deeper

1. What does it mean to live a holy life? And why would you want to live that way?
2. How can you grow in holiness?
3. Ask the Holy Spirit if there is an area in your life that He wants to sanctify and transform. Try to imagine what that area would look like sanctified.
4. Is there an area in your life where you want change but that you know is not changing? Who could you ask for help so that you can grow?

Meditation Verses:

Psalm 16:6
1 John 2:15
1 John 1:9

12

Loving Well

Some years ago, I met a pastoral couple who impressed me. Somehow, I got to speak at their church, which was located in a very small town close to the U.S. border with Canada. It seemed to be in the middle of nowhere. We had a great service, and I was encouraged by what the Lord did that morning as we gathered together to meet Him.

Later that day, I got to spend some time with the pastors. They were telling me how the Lord had led them from afar to come to this church, how it had been a mess, and how the last ten years God had been bringing healing and restoration to the community. Now, there was life and growth and an excitement in the air over what God was doing in their midst. But I have to be honest with you. This church didn't seem successful to me at first glance. Pastoring a little church in the middle of nowhere is not my dream. And I thought to myself, *I'm glad I don't live here.*

Yet, there was something about these pastors—something that made them very attractive to me. I loved being around them. One of the first things I couldn't help but notice was that they were very much in love with each other. They had grown children and had been married for many years, but they were behaving like kids who had just fallen in love. I don't think I have ever seen an older couple appear so young and in love with each other.

When they talked about the community they were serving, it was very evident they really loved its people, too. When I was talking to the wife, she got emotional telling me of an encounter she had had with God in which He had shown her how much He loved her. It changed her life. It had filled her heart with love and made her a lover.

I could feel the pleasure of God over this couple. They loved well. It was contagious, and it left me rethinking what success was. I wanted to be like them. I realized after meeting them that I'd rather love well than look good.

Some time after visiting with them, I was at a funeral of a man from my community. He had been a part of my church for many years. At seventy years old, he and his wife had five children and a whole bunch of grandchildren. Many people attended his funeral. He was a painter, but that was not what he was mostly known for. Person after person testified about how this man's love had impacted their lives. He was a man who was a real father in the community. Young and old were changed by his love. He greatly loved both God and people. And again, I thought, *This is what success looks like: loving well.*

Commanded to Love

Peter wrote, "Above all things have fervent love for one another" (1 Pet. 4:8). And Paul wrote, "And walk in love, as Christ also has loved us and given Himself for us, an offering and a sacrifice to God for a sweet-smelling aroma" (Eph. 5:2).

When we get to know the love of God, it will help us love ourselves, and it will also help us love people. The first commandment leads to the second commandment.

Jesus said to him, "'You shall love the LORD your God with all your heart, with all your soul, and with all your mind.' This is the first and great commandment. And the second is like it: 'You shall love your neighbor as yourself.'" (Mt. 22:37–39)

In my teenage years, I would go on YWAM (Youth with a Mission) mission trips every summer. One summer, we went to southern Europe for several weeks with about thirty teenagers. I loved the traveling, the new experiences, making friends, and seeing God move. There was one problem, though. A girl. Her name was "Sarah." And I couldn't get along with her at all. She annoyed me to no end. She always made silly jokes that I thought were not funny, and then she'd laugh really hard at them. As a young teenager, I had already learned that I shouldn't be the one who laughs the loudest about my own jokes. Not cool. And when she laughed, she would snort like a pig.

At last, I decided I needed to talk to one of the staff. I figured it was a leader's job to fix things that were wrong. So, I told the male staffer that there was a problem on our team—Sarah. I explained what was wrong with her and how she was not good for our team. The leader patiently heard me out and then responded with a suggestion. He said, "Daniel, why don't you start praying for her, and ask God to show you how He feels about her?"

This was definitely not what I wanted to hear. There were other options. He could have offered to talk to her and rebuke her, he could have forbidden her to tell those jokes, or he could have sent her back home. His suggestion didn't sound like a solution. But what could I say? "No, I am not going to pray about it"?

No, I couldn't say that. I figured I'd have to tough it out and pray for her.

That night I went to bed. I do that most nights.

The guys all slept in the main auditorium of a little church on our air mattresses, and the girls slept in a classroom down the hallway. As I was lying there, I prayed for Sarah. I don't remember my exact wording, but I asked God to intervene and fix Sarah. It felt somewhat good to be partnering with God in restoring a broken person. Oh, and I also asked God to show me how He saw her.

Early the next morning, the guys and I woke up to screams from the girls. Their screams were coming from the hallway. Several of us rushed out to see what was up, only to find out that Sarah had died in her sleep.

I am just kidding. She didn't die. We all just woke up fine. I'll tell you what did happen, though. As a few days went by and I prayed for her every day, instead of praying that she would change, I think I started to change. God was really answering my prayer, only differently than I had expected. My immature heart changed, and a love for Sarah grew inside me. I actually started to enjoy her. In fact, her jokes became funny to me. Her jokes would make both of us laugh. She still snorted like a pig, but it didn't bother me anymore. She was happy, and I embraced that was simply how she laughed. At the end of the mission trip, we said goodbye, and I realized she had become one of my favorite people on the team.

Now, I know this was a little silly, but this was an important experience for me. I started learning God loves anyone, and I can do the same when I tap into His emotions toward the one He loves. Most of the time, we don't want to seek God for His heart for people around us, especially people we don't like. It is easier to reject or ignore or hate them. And many times, the people around us who need love the most ask in the worst kind of ways. And we'd rather not choose to love.

Henry and Richard Blackaby said, "A test of your love for God is to examine your love for others."[1]

It is so confronting when we realize the truth of something Andrew Murray said, "Our love for God is measured by our everyday interaction with men and the love it displays."[2]

But God, who even loved us while we were His enemies, loves it when we love the people that He loves so much.

We were created to be connected relationally to others. We don't do well alone. No one thrives in isolation, because we were all made for community. After God created Adam, He said that it was not good for man to be alone. And it is still not good for men and women to be alone.

Our primary need is to know and experience God's love and acceptance of us personally, but after that comes the need to be loved and accepted by people. That is just how God made us. When God gave us the first and second commandments, to love Him and to love our neighbor, He knew we would be most happy when we did them both.

The Value of Others

Again, we don't do well alone. We don't thrive in isolation. Our God is relational in nature, and we were made in His image. We need other people, and that is as it should be.

The goal is not to be self-sufficient. Much of the grace of God in our lives comes to us through the people God places in our lives. That's how He wants it.

Here's some wisdom from Solomon: "Though one may be overpowered by another, two can withstand him. And a threefold cord is not quickly broken" (Eccl. 4:12). Solomon here compares the person who stands alone to the one who stands in friendship. The person who is isolated lives a dangerous life. Alone you may get overpowered. You are limited by and left to your own strength and ability. When you fight alone, you are very vulnerable to the attacks of the enemy. And attacks will come. You can't expect peace when you've declared war. But as Solomon explains, when you are relationally connected, you can defend yourself from attack. You will not be overpowered. It gets real hard for the enemy to take you out. When you are isolated and you stumble or hurt, you hurt alone. You mourn your defeats alone. Danny Silk said, "Addictions are cycles that emerged in our lives when we cannot reduce our pain and anxiety through loving, intimate, connections with people."³

In loneliness, defeat tends to turn into shame, leading to more isolation. Furthermore, we tend to get stuck desperately grasping for anything to escape the negative emotions. We can get addicted to what helps us cope but really doesn't do us any good. It does the opposite; it damages us and our relationships.

Listen to what the apostle Peter tells us: "Be alert and of sober mind. Your enemy the devil prowls around like a roaring lion looking for someone to devour" (1 Pet. 5:8 NIV). The devil is compared to a lion. That makes a lot of sense to me. Living in Africa, we have seen them: wild beasts who kill the weakest animal, the one who falls behind the herd, with no mercy.

Peter warns his readers that the devil actively looks for someone to devour. Don't let this cause you to be afraid. It should simply help you be aware of the adversary's pursuit. The apostle Paul understood the dynamics of the enemy, as well, and he gave his spiritual son some fatherly advice: "Pursue righteousness, faith, love and peace, along with those who call on the Lord out of a pure heart" (2 Tim. 2:22 NIV). I love Paul's advice to Timothy not to do life with God on your own. We should pursue God with those who are prayerful and wholehearted.

Growth in God must be pursued in the company of like-minded followers of Jesus. You grow with others. Godly community and friendship are so incredibly important. In fact, I believe that to a very large degree your success in life and God are determined by the quality of your relationships.

Relationships, though, are risky because no one is perfect. And people's imperfections can hurt us. When I was younger, something about becoming a monk appealed to me. I often imagined myself living in a little hut on a mountain, in the middle of nowhere, just me and God. I loved God but had a hard time really relating to people, so this seemed like a great solution. And it sounded spiritual, too.

I imagined I would hang out with God all day, experiencing Him, and avoid all the risk and drama of relating to other human beings. I didn't think all people were difficult, though. Quite the opposite. I felt that the problem was mostly me. I was ashamed of myself. I didn't think I acted like the person I was supposed to be. I felt broken and embarrassed by my sins and spiritual immaturity.

When Adam and Eve messed up, they went into hiding and covered their nakedness. We like to do the same when things go wrong: hide, cover up our mistakes, and when we see someone, pretend like all is well. We think if we act as if we're really spiritual, then no one will know how messed up we are. We wear a mask. When you wear a mask, however, it is only the mask that receives the love. The real you will never experience the love you desperately need.

Like Adam and Eve, we try to hide ourselves from God. We dress up like Esau to try to earn the Father's blessing. We pretend like we are someone other than our true selves, hoping to fool God into liking us.

For most of my life, the culture around me has been telling me to be a real man. It says I have to be independent, self-sufficient, and in control. Culture says I should withhold personal information and be competitive and physically tough. But that's not really a definition of manhood. And it's a very superficial picture of courage.

It actually takes a lot of courage to let yourself be known for who you really are. When I encounter hardship, I like to keep the struggle to myself. I'd rather share with others what's going well in my life, but we tend to get stuck when we don't risk connecting with other people.

My eldest son has broken bones several times. One day, he broke both wrists at the same time. After both his arms were put in casts, for the first few days he could do almost nothing. He became very dependent on Marlies and me to take care of him. We fed and clothed him, and even helped him use the bathroom.

Sometimes, when a part of us breaks, we need help. The Beatles sang it, "Help, I need somebody!" And we have to learn to receive help when it's given or offered to us.

When I hit the wall as a missionary in Africa, a dear friend of mine who pastors a church in Canada invited my family to come visit his community for some time to heal. The church paid for all our airfare and also gave us a car to use and a house to stay in for those two months. The church even arranged for me to talk to a counselor. I appreciate counselors, but I didn't like needing one myself. I remember sitting in the pastor's office and crying. I told him I hated this. I hated that I couldn't do anything for him or the church. I felt so empty, and I couldn't stand being needy and not useful. My friend gently told me this was a time to receive. He encouraged me to surrender to that season.

It's humbling to receive. I wanted to resist. "You shall never wash my feet!" Peter said to Jesus when Jesus wanted to serve His friend (Jn. 13:8).

The first Sunday in church, my pastor friend called my family up on the stage. He wanted to tell the whole congregation about us. As I stood there looking at all the people in the congregation, I felt embarrassed on the inside about where I was in life. The pastor introduced us, saying, these are missionary heroes of mine. And then he bragged on us. He told everyone I loved steak. What followed were two months of this community loving on us and feeding us a lifetime of incredible steak. There were days that we would have people inviting us over to their homes for food and fellowship for all three meals of the day!

And, then, Thanksgiving happened. Being from the Netherlands, we had never experienced it before. We literally had four Thanksgiving meals in a row—with different people! I didn't even understand what the holiday was about, but it became immediately clear to us that fellowshipping around large amounts of food was at the center of it. Let me tell you, we went for it. By the time we sat down for the fourth Thanksgiving meal, I was sweating gravy and needed the fire department to help me get out of my chair.

The beautiful thing was we found healing being real with people who chose to love us. You know what else was beautiful? The huge steaks! Both were beautiful.

We choose to love people. But we also need to choose to allow people to love us. It is a powerful experience we all long for when people love us with the knowledge of both our good and broken parts. To experience this, we have to come out of hiding. With wisdom, we choose to let someone know who we really are.

For the longest time, I didn't want to be known fully. I wanted people to keep at a distance because I was afraid that, if they saw who I was, they'd reject me. I even struggled with keeping Marlies at a distance at times, afraid she would not love me anymore. I was concerned that leaders would write me off if they knew the real me.

The opposite happened, however. The truth is, the more we let people know us in the context of healthy friendships, the deeper we will feel loved.

God's love transforms us. It gives us the ability to love others. Already secure in His love, we then have the confidence to let others love us. We no longer desperately seek to prove ourselves to others since we have found affirmation and acceptance in God.

God made you, and He thinks the world of you. You are infinitely valuable, and He decided to place you on this earth. He wanted to write His story with you in it. He wants you to know today that there is a place for you here, and He wants you to take it. You have the right to be here. And He doesn't want you looking like the next guy. He wants you to be you. So, go for it! Be yourself. Don't be ashamed. God is proud of you. Let people feel the weight of who you are, and engage. Come out of hiding. Step into the light. Pursue the hearts of your friends, and let them know yours—because you are worth knowing.[4]

Going Deeper

1. Think of a few people you know who really love you. How do they make you feel loved?
2. If your love for God can be measured by how well you love those around you, how do you think you are doing?
3. Do you feel relationally connected to other people, or is your life more marked by loneliness and isolation?
4. How do you think feeling secure in God's love for you personally will help you love others?

Meditation Verses:

1 Peter 4:8
Ephesians 5:2
2 Timothy 2:22

13

Loving God

I once read something Donald Miller said, "If we knew how much God loved us and was for us, we'd talk to Him all day long."[1] This reminds me of the best advice I ever received. It came from a tall, German man. I met him at a Vineyard Worship Conference held in the Netherlands. I had responded to an invitation to come forward for prayer to be baptized with the Holy Spirit. This man prayed for me, and God powerfully met me that night. Afterward, the man told me to talk to God—about everything. He told me that, if it mattered to me, God would want to hear about it. And so I did what he said.

No advice had an impact on my relationship with God as much as that man's did. I was a socially awkward teenager at the time, who was not great at conversing with people. The idea of simply talking to God about stuff made sense to me. I remember walking around and silently processing everything that happened in my conversations with God—like He was my best friend who was physically walking right next to me. I would tell Him about the food I enjoyed, the pretty girl that made me nervous, my lonely feelings, the normal stuff a teenager experiences. I realized that, the more I talked to God, the more I experienced Him.

Sometimes, I sensed God spoke back to me. Sometimes, I felt like He was right there with me. In fact, I believed it. Day by day, I started to develop a relationship with Him. Then, I had to learn to drive a car.

In the Netherlands, it is very expensive to get your driver's license as you have to pay a lot of money for both the lessons and the exam itself. Before I had my first lesson, I talked to God about it. This was going to be a big deal, and I wanted Him to be a part of it. I asked Him to meet me in all of it. After about two-thousand-dollars'-worth of lessons, I still managed to drive through a red light twice within one minute during a lesson. Needless to say, I was not doing well. But my instructor told me to try to take an exam anyway. I did, and of course I failed. That meant more lessons.

A few months later, my instructor told me to try again. The evening before, I was at home in my room praying. As I was lying on my bed talking to God about how nervous I was about taking the exam, I felt God telling me that I would pass. I got off my bed and was so excited! I called a friend and told him that God had just told me I would pass my exam the next day. He loved it, and then suggested we should act in faith upon what God had spoken by telling more people that I would pass the exam. That sounded right, so we both called a few other people to announce I would get my driver's license the next day.

My parents weren't home that evening. They were at the neighbor's house for their weekly church small-group gathering. So, I went to the neighbor's home and knocked on the door. The neighbor let me in, and I asked if I could tell the group something exciting God had told me. My parents were a little surprised to see me there, but with conviction I announced to all of them that God had told me I would pass my exam the next day.

I slept great that night. The next morning, I realized I needed some cake to celebrate. I went out and bought a cake in faith. Later that day, I went for the exam. The examiner told me where to go and what to do as I was driving. I was still a bit nervous. In the Netherlands, when you take an exam, if the examiner at any moment needs to intervene by hitting the brakes or grabbing the steering wheel because of danger, that is always an automatic fail. Sure enough, toward the end of the exam, the examiner had to intervene. He slammed the brakes. I didn't want to look at him, so I kept going. Internally, all the while, I thanked God over and over again that I would still pass.

Soon, we got out of the car, and the examiner took me inside. I kept praying in my heart, *Thank You, God, for letting me pass. Thank You for letting me pass.* The examiner looked at me and with a deep sigh said, "Well, you've passed." I went home happy. I celebrated and ate the cake! I loved that God was so much a part of such a normal thing.

Another moment with God that I treasure occurred after I ministered in the Netherlands at a youth conference. At the end of the conference, I was dropped off at the airport to fly back to Kenya where we lived at that time. I had some time to kill, so I browsed some of the shops, among them a watch store. (I've never understood why people buy ridiculously expensive watches at airports.) I was looking at a few dive watches. I love scuba diving, and for a while I had wanted a Citizen dive watch. But the model I wanted was a very costly watch we couldn't afford. For two years, every birthday and Christmas, I would joke with my wife about wanting that watch. As I was looking at "my watch" in the airport store, I realized I would never buy it. Then, I got an idea. I could ask God to send someone to buy it for me. So, I did.

I waited around a while to give God the opportunity to send His person. No one came to offer to buy me a watch, though. I realized what I was doing was a little silly, so I walked away. But I thought maybe God did want to gift me the watch and figured His person may have needed to come from the other side of the airport and just hadn't had time to get there yet. So, I went back, looked around, and made some awkward eye contact with people who looked rich, but nothing happened. I walked out again. In a short while, I came back for a third time, wanting to make sure I gave God all the time He needed to set this up for me. Again, nothing happened, and I decided to board my plane home.

The next day, a couple from the Netherlands came to visit us. We didn't know them at the time. They knew some of our family and had heard about our work and wanted to come and see it. They arrived in the evening and, being tired from the trip, went to bed quickly.

The following morning, I stood in the kitchen leaning against the countertop when the male visitor walked in. He said, "Daniel, God told me to give you my watch." He handed me his watch. It was a Citizen dive watch. Incredible! Only two days earlier, I had looked at this watch in the shop at the airport in the Netherlands. Though this man had never made a dive in his life, he loved good watches and had purchased it.

I was amazed that God would care about stuff like this.

Another friend of mine loves fishing—a lot. And when he was younger, he attended a meeting where a man he didn't know prayed for him. The man said that God had spoken to him and was asking a question: "Can I come fishing with you?"

I love stories like these. They show us how much God wants to be a part of our lives. He is not involved solely in our church meetings or Bible studies. He is with us always and wants to be included in the everyday stuff of life.

When you read the Gospels, you find that Jesus was always talking to His Father. Although there is not that much recorded about His childhood, from His baptism onward we get an intimate look into His life. We find that after Jesus was baptized, He prayed, the heavens opened, and the Father declared His love over Him (Lk. 3:21–22). Then, He went into the wilderness for forty days to pray and fast (Lk. 4:1). A while after He came out, He spent the whole night on a mountain in prayer before choosing His disciples (Lk. 6:12). Next, His ministry really picked up. He was very busy, going about doing good. During the demanding days of ministering to great multitudes, He still withdrew to connect with His Father in prayer as we read in the following verses:

> And when He had sent the multitudes away, He went up on the mountain by Himself to pray. (Mt. 14:23)
>
> He Himself often withdrew into the wilderness and prayed. (Lk. 5:16)
>
> Now in the morning, having risen a long while before daylight, He went out and departed to a solitary place; and there He prayed. (Mk. 1:35)

Jesus thanked the Father for food (Jn. 6:11). He prayed with His disciples and for His disciples (Lk. 9:28; Jn. 17:9).

At the end of Jesus' life, before He was arrested, He wrestled in prayer about what awaited Him: "He had offered up prayers and supplications, with vehement cries and tears to Him" (Heb. 5:7). Jesus knew what it was like to be alone with the Father and cry out from the deep places of His heart. In this most challenging time of His life, He asked His disciples to stand with Him in prayer (Mt. 26:36; Lk. 22:39–41). Even in the very last moments of His life, as He hung on the cross, He was talking to His Father, asking Him to forgive the people who were crucifying Him (Lk. 23:34). His last words were, "'"Father, into Your hands I commit My spirit"'" (Lk. 23:46).

After Jesus rose from the dead and made His way back home to the right hand of the Father, He was still talking to His Father (Heb. 7:25). And He always will.

One time, when Jesus had just finished praying, a disciple asked Him, "'Lord, teach us to pray'" (Lk. 11:1). They wanted what He had.

So, Jesus taught them to pray. And He teaches us today, because He wants us to have what He has. He wants us to be one with the Father as He and the Father are one (Jn. 17:20–23). It is what we were made for—intimate unity with God. God never called us to a religion. He called us to Himself—to enjoy intimate friendship with Him. It is the joy of the Christian life.

Many have gone before us and experienced intimacy with God. For example, it was said of Noah that he was a righteous man who enjoyed a close relationship with God (Gen. 6:9). God spoke to Moses face to face, as a man would speak to his friend (Ex. 33:11). When Job went through his time of testing, he thought of how things used to be and how he missed the time when God's intimate friendship blessed his house (Job 29:4). And King David was described as a man after God's own heart. He was consumed with the Lord's presence. He said, "One thing I have desired of the Lord, that will I seek: that I may dwell in the house of the Lord all the days of my life, to behold the beauty of the Lord, and to inquire in His temple" (Ps. 27:4).

Andrew Murray pursued the same. As you may remember from chapter 1, he said, "May not a single moment of my life be spent outside the light, love, and joy of God's presence. And not a moment without the entire surrender of myself as a vessel for Him to fill full of His Spirit and His love."[2]

When John Fletcher (1729–1785), an Anglican minister in England, passed away, his wife, Mary, said of him:

> It was his constant endeavor to maintain an uninterrupted sense of the presence of God . . . Indeed he both acted, and spoke, and thought, as under the eye of God. And thus setting God always before him, he remained unmoved in all occurrences . . . Sometimes he took his journeys alone, but above a thousand miles I have traveled with him, during which neither change of company, place, nor the variety of circumstances which naturally occur in traveling ever seemed to make the least difference in his firm attention

to the presence of God . . . And I can say with truth, all his union with me was so intermingled with prayer and praise that every activity and every meal was, as it were, perfumed therewith.[3]

This is not only for Bible characters or heroes of the faith. Jeanne Guyon once said, "Most Christians do not feel that *they* have been called to a deep, inward relationship to their Lord. But we have all been called to the depths of Christ just as surely as we have been called to salvation."[4]

And Psalm 145:18 assures us, "The LORD is near to all who call upon Him." You and I are both called to experience His nearness and to cultivate friendship with Him. How do we do this?

Developing Friendship with God

Well, it begins with faith. It is hard to exaggerate how important faith is in relating to God. We must approach Him with faith in who He is and what He has done.

If your trust in God is damaged, your fellowship with Him will be greatly hindered. Trust is a basic building block of relationships, and if lost, you shut down on the inside. You close your heart. You can do the same thing with others. You automatically keep people you don't trust at a distance. I encourage you to not shut down but believe that God is good, that He welcomes your nearness, and that He is a loving Father who loves to hear His children. When you talk to Him, don't think you are bothering someone who is very busy with more important things. He always has time for you.

When we draw near to God, He draws near to us. You don't have to twist His arm to make Him respond. You don't have to impress Him. You don't have to say all the things you think you're supposed to say. When you talk to God, just be real with Him. Your Father, who sees you, will reward you. He will never leave. He is always there.

Have a boldness before God rooted in Jesus' accomplishment on the cross. We don't relate to God on the basis of our own righteousness; we come in the name of Jesus. You don't have to earn your approval before God; instead, put your trust in what Jesus has already done to give you right standing before Him. It is not the sacrifice you make; it is the sacrifice you trust. Meaning, your acceptance is not because of a sacrifice you make; it is because you trust the sacrifice He made.

Don't view intimacy with God as something you have to earn. Rather, see it as something Jesus made available for you and offers you. Of course, to experience it, we have to respond to this offer. But don't see it as something you have to earn the right to enter. It is your inheritance as a child of God.

Timothy Keller says, "The only person who dares wake up a king at 3:00 AM for a glass of water is a child. We have that kind of access."[5] Your access to God is through faith in Jesus Christ. But your greatest practical tool to cultivate friendship with Him is His Word. God's Word given to you is His invitation to get to know Him. The knowledge of God is the substance of our intimacy with God. Just think about it—the people you are closest to, you know the most about.

The Bible leads us into the knowledge of God. But don't read the Bible only for information. Bible knowledge does not equal knowing God. Let it lead you into relationship with a real Person. That happens primarily when we take the Scriptures and bring them into conversation with God.

Let the Bible give you the conversational material for your prayer life. This is not a new idea. For thousands of years, men and women have prayed the Bible, including the early church (see Acts 4:24–31). Go ahead and try it. Get alone with God and your Bible. Maybe start with Psalm 23, and turn it into a prayer to God. The psalms are just perfect for this. Use the language of the biblical author and speak it back to God. When you pray the Bible, you'll find things to agree with, to thank God for, and to apply to your own life, and you'll never run out of things to talk to God about. Of course, not every single verse in the Bible lends itself to this even though many do. Sometimes, you have to read more verses to get the idea explained in the passage.

Another good idea to get started is to go back to chapter 4 of this book and highlight or underline all the verses there. They came from my own prayer list of scriptures that I have prayed over and over again to grow in my understanding of what God the Father is like.

It is amazing that we have the ear of heaven, that God Himself hears us and responds to the very words we speak. What a privilege to be His child, and what a joy to know this love. We can say with the psalmist: "You will show me the path of life; in Your presence is fullness of joy; at Your right hand are pleasures forevermore" (Ps. 16:11).

Be confident in His love. He really loves you—right now.

Going Deeper

1. When you pray, do you tend to say what you think you are supposed to say, or do you feel like you are genuinely speaking from your heart to a real person?
2. What everyday areas of your life would you like to experience God's presence in?
3. What are things you can do to help you talk more to God?
4. Take some time to pray, but before you begin, why don't you take a few minutes just to consider the reality that the God who knows you the best and who loves you the most is real, sees you, and listens to you.

Meditation Verses:

Luke 5:16
Psalm 27:4
Psalm 16:11

Acknowledgments

Marlies—I am so happy that you love me. You show me every day what it looks like to love with all your heart and to live surrendered to God.

Aiden, Leona, and David—I am SO proud of you. You have no idea how much joy you give me.

Mike Bickle—I am so grateful for your leadership. Thank you for being such a great example of wholeheartedness to me and my family.

Hendre Coetzee—you gave me the motivation to write this book.

Jeff and Kathryn Culver—thank you for providing a most beautiful place to write and for sharing your lives with us.

Rimoun Hanna—you made it possible for me to write this book.

Edie Mourey—you're a pro. Thank you for all your work in making my thoughts and stories a book.

Amy Peterson—you are such a joy to work with. You are so kind, wise, and creative. Thank you for caring about this book.

Mattheus van der Steen—your friendship means the world to me.

Thank you to all the IHOPKC singers and musicians who faithfully declare the beauty of the Lord by day and by night.

Notes

Introduction

1. Quoted in Paul Dwight Moody and Arthur Percy Fitt, *The Shorter Life of D. L. Moody,* vol. 1 (Chicago: The Bible Institute Colportage Association, n.d.), 67.
2. Ibid., 67.
3. Winkie Pratney, *Revival: Principles to Change the World* (Pensacola: Christian Life Books, 1984), 140.
4. James Gilchrist Lawson, *Deeper Experiences of Famous Christians* (Anderson, IN: The Warner Press, 1911), 348.
5. S. B. Shaw, *The Great Revival in Wales* (Chicago: S. B. Shaw, 1905), 11.
6. Brennan Manning, *Ruthless Trust: The Ragamuffin's Path to God* (New York: HarperCollins, 2000), 148.

Chapter 1: It Takes God to Love God

1. R. A. Torrey, *How to Bring Men to Christ* (Chicago: Fleming H. Revell Company, 1893), 21–22.
2. Mike Bickle, "Loving Jesus: The First Commandment Established in First Place," ihopkc.org, International House of Prayer of Kansas City (Free Teaching Library), http://www.ihopkc.org.edgesuite.net/notes/2016_04/Loving%20Jesus-%20First%20Commandment%20Established%20in%20First%20Place%20%28PFJ%29.pdf/, accessed May 8, 2019.
3. J. I. Packer, *Knowing God* (London: Hodder & Stoughton, 1973), 25–26.
4. W. M. Douglas, *Andrew Murray and His Message* (London: C. Tinling & Co., Ltd., 1926), 116.

Chapter 2: The Wrong Picture

1. J. I. Packer, *Knowing God* (Downers Grove: InterVarsity Press, 1975, 1993), 200.
2. David Pawson, *A Commentary on Jude* (Ashford: Anchor Recordings Ltd., 2013), 54–55.
3. David Pawson, *Introduction to Romans*, undated recording, MP3 audio file.

Chapter 3: Defined by the Father

1. Brennan Manning, *Abba's Child: The Cry of the Heart for Intimate Belonging* (Colorado Springs: NavPress, 2015), 4.
2. Jack and Trisha Frost, *Spiritual Slavery to Spiritual Sonship: Your Destiny Awaits You* (Shippensburg: Destiny Image Publishers, Inc., 2016), 69.
3. Paraphrased from Bianca Juárez Olthoff, *Play with Fire: Discovering Fierce Faith, Unquenchable Passion, and a Life-Giving God.* (Grand Rapids: Zondervan, 2016), 119.
4. Henri Nouwen (@HenriNouwen), "If you know you are Beloved of God, you can live with an enormous amount of success and an enormous amount of failure without losing your identity, because your identity is that you are the Beloved," Twitter, October 7, 2018, 6:59 p.m., https://twitter.com/henrinouwen/status/1049117081877340165?lang=en.
5. David Lomas, *The Truest Thing About You* (Colorado Springs: David C. Cook, 2014), 36.

Chapter 4: The Father Revealed

1. Jim Reimann, ed., *Morning by Morning: The Devotions of Charles Spurgeon* (Grand Rapids: Zondervan, 2008), 3.

NOTES

Chapter 5: The Father's Affirmation

1. Anonymous report from a Muslim-majority nation. Author unknown.

Chapter 10: A Different Perspective

1. A. J. Broomhall, *Hudson Taylor and China's Open Century, Book Four: Survivor's Pact* (London: Hodder & Stoughton and Overseas Missionary Fellowship, 1984), 154.
2. Charles H. Spurgeon, *Collected Works, Vol. 1* (Brandon: Revelation Insight Publishing, 2010), 124.
3. Robert J. Morgan, *Then Sings My Soul: 150 of the World's Greatest Hymn Stories* (Nashville: Thomas Nelson, 2003), 184–185.
4. Words to "It Is Well with My Soul" by Horatio G. Spafford, 1873.
5. Portions of chapter 10 adapted from: Daniel Hoogteijling, "Five Keys for Loving God Despite Discouragement," International House of Prayer of Kansas City, May 31, 2017, https://www.ihop-kc.org/resources/blog/five-keys-for-loving-god-despite-discouragement/ (accessed October 17, 2019).

Chapter 11: Love, the Way of Holiness

1. Albert M. Wells, *Inspiring Quotations: Contemporary and Classical* (Nashville: Thomas Nelson, 1988) 88, #1121. As cited in Michael L. Brown, *Go and Sin No More: A Call to Holiness* (Ventura: Regal Books, 1999), 237.
2. C. S. Lewis, *Mere Christianity* (London: HarperCollins Publishers, 1997), 53.
3. Brother Lawrence, *The Practice of the Presence of God* (New Kensington: Whitaker House, 1982), 15–16.
4. Stephen J. Rossetti, *When the Lion Roars* (Notre Dame: Ave Maria Press, 2003), back cover.

Chapter 12: Loving Well

1. Henry and Richard Blackaby, *Experiencing God, Day by Day* (Nashville: B & H Publishing Group, 2006), January 12.

2. Andrew Murray, *Humility: The Beauty of Holiness* (Abbotsford: Aneko Press, 2016), 32.

3. Danny Silk (@dannyleesilk), "Addictions are cycles that emerged in our lives when we cannot reduce our pain and anxiety through loving, intimate, connections with people," Twitter, April 30, 2015.

4. Portions of chapter 12 adapted from: Daniel Hoogteijling, "Five Keys for Loving God Despite Discouragement," International House of Prayer of Kansas City, May 31, 2017, https://www.ihop-kc.org/resources/blog/five-keys-for-loving-god-despite-discouragement/ (accessed October 17, 2019).

Chapter 13: Loving God

1. Donald Miller, "If we knew how much God loved us and was for us, we'd talk to Him all day long," Facebook, January 19, 2014, https://www.facebook.com/donaldmillerwords/posts/10151830944541721.

2. W. M. Douglas, *Andrew Murray and His Message* (London: C. Tinling & Co., Ltd., 1926), 116.

3. David Lyle Jeffrey, ed., *English Spirituality in the Age of Wesley* (Grand Rapids: Wm. B. Eerdmans Publishing Co., 1987), 349–350.

4. Jeanne Guyon, *Experiencing the Depths of Jesus Christ*, Library of Spiritual Classics, vol. 2 (Sargent: SeedSowers, 1975), 1.

5. Timothy Keller (@timkellernyc), "The only person who dares wake up a king at 3:00 AM for a glass of water is a child. We have that kind of access," Twitter, April 27, 2019, 8:30 a.m., https://twitter.com/timkellernyc/status/1122161008963878913.

International House *of* Prayer
MISSIONS BASE OF KANSAS CITY

24/7 Live Worship with Prayer since 1999

On September 19, 1999, a prayer meeting began that continues to this day; from dawn to dusk and through the watches of the night, by the grace of God, prayer and worship have continued twenty-four hours a day, seven days a week.

Learn more at ihopkc.org/about

Unceasing is a monthly subscription to our exclusive, growing library of spontaneous worship recorded live at the International House of Prayer. Every month we add our best songs, prophetic moments, intercession cycles, and instrumental selahs.

Learn more at unceasingworship.com

International House of Prayer Missions Base, 3535 E. Red Bridge Road, Kansas City, MO 64137
(816) 763-0200 | info@ihopkc.org

INTERNATIONAL HOUSE of PRAYER UNIVERSITY

MINISTRY • MUSIC • MEDIA • MISSIONS

··

ENCOUNTER GOD. DO HIS WORKS. CHANGE THE WORLD.

ihopkc.org/ihopu

··

International House of Prayer University (IHOPU) is a full-time Bible school which exists to equip this generation in the Word and in the power of the Holy Spirit for the bold proclamation of the Lord Jesus and His return.

As part of the International House of Prayer, our Bible school is built around the centrality of the Word and 24/7 prayer with worship, equipping students in the Word and the power of the Spirit for the bold proclamation of the Lord Jesus and His kingdom. Training at IHOPU forms not only minds but also lifestyle and character, to sustain students for a life of obedience, humility, and anointed service in the kingdom. Our curriculum combines in-depth biblical training with discipleship, practical service, outreach, and works of compassion.

IHOPU is for students who long to encounter Jesus. With schools of ministry, music, media, and missions, our one- to four-year certificate and diploma programs prepare students to engage in the Great Commission and obey Jesus' commandments to love God and people.

> "What Bible School has 'prayer' on its curriculum? The most important thing a man can study is the prayer part of the Book. But where is this taught?
>
> Let us strip off the last bandage and declare that many of our presidents and teachers do not pray, shed no tears, know no travail. Can they teach what they do not know?"
>
> –Leonard Ravenhill, *Why Revival Tarries*

International House of Prayer University, 12901 S. US Highway 71, Grandview, MO 64030
(816) 763-0243 | info@ihopu.org

International House *of* Prayer
INTERNSHIPS

INTRO TO IHOPKC • FIRE IN THE NIGHT • ONE THING INTERNSHIP
SIMEON COMPANY • HOPE CITY INTERNSHIP

ihopkc.org/internships

Internships exist to see people equipped with the Word of God, ministering in the power of the Holy Spirit, engaged in intercession, and committed to outreach and service.

Our five internships are three to six months long and accommodate all seasons of life. The purpose of the internships is to further prepare individuals of all ages as intercessors, worshipers, messengers, singers, and musicians for the work of the kingdom. While each internship has a distinctive age limit, length, and schedule, they all share the same central training components: corporate prayer and worship meetings, classroom instruction, practical ministry experience, outreach, and relationship-building.

Biblical teaching in all of the internships focuses on intimacy with Jesus, ministry in the power of the Holy Spirit, the forerunner ministry, evangelizing the lost, justice, and outreach. Interns also receive practical, hands-on training in the prophetic and healing ministries.

Upon successful completion of a six-month internship or two three-month tracks, some will stay and apply to join IHOPKC staff.

Our IHOPKC Leadership Team

Our leadership team of over a hundred and fifty men and women, with diversity of experience, background, and training, represent twenty countries and thirty denominations and oversee eighty-five departments on our missions base. With a breadth of experience in pastoral ministry, missions work, education, and the marketplace, this team's training in various disciplines includes over forty master's degrees and ten doctorates.

International House of Prayer Missions Base, 3535 E. Red Bridge Road, Kansas City, MO 64137
(816) 763-0200 | internships@ihopkc.org

MIKE BICKLE
TEACHING LIBRARY
— Free Teaching & Resource Library —

This International House of Prayer resource library, encompassing more than thirty years of Mike's teaching ministry, provides access to hundreds of resources in various formats, including streaming video, downloadable video, and audio, accompanied by study notes and transcripts, absolutely free of charge.

You will find some of Mike's most requested titles, including *The Gospel of Grace*; *The First Commandment*; *Jesus, Our Magnificent Obsession*; *Romans: Theology of Holy Passion*; *The Sermon on the Mount: The Kingdom Lifestyle*; and much more.

We encourage you to freely copy any of these teachings to share with others or use in any way: "our copyright is the right to copy." Older messages are being prepared and uploaded from Mike's teaching archives, and all new teachings are added immediately.

Visit mikebickle.org

International House of Prayer Missions Base, 3535 E. Red Bridge Road, Kansas City, MO 64137
(816) 763-0200 | info@ihopkc.org | ihopkc.org